# REAL CAJUN

# REAL CAJUN

## RUSTIC HOME COOKING
## FROM DONALD LINK'S LOUISIANA

### DONALD LINK

WITH PAULA DISBROWE

PHOTOGRAPHS BY CHRIS GRANGER

CLARKSON POTTER/PUBLISHERS

NEW YORK

Copyright © 2009 by Donald Link
Photographs © 2009 by Chris Granger

All rights reserved.
Published in the United States by Clarkson Potter/Publishers, an imprint of
the Crown Publishing Group, a division of Random House, Inc., New York.
www.crownpublishing.com
www.clarksonpotter.com

Clarkson Potter is a trademark and Potter
with colophon is a registered trademark of
Random House, Inc.

Library of Congress Cataloging-in-Publication Data
Link, Donald.
    Real Cajun: Rustic home cooking from Donald Link's Louisiana / Donald Link. — 1st ed.
        p.   cm.
    Includes bibliographical references.
    1. Cookery, American—Louisiana style.   2. Cookery, Cajun.   3. Cochon Restaurant
(New Orleans, LA.)   I. Title.
TX715.2.L68L56   2009
641.59763—dc22                                                2008036989

ISBN 978-0-307-39581-8

Printed in China

Design by Marysarah Quinn

10  9  8  7  6  5  4  3  2  1

FIRST EDITION

TO MY KIDS, CASSIDY AND NICHOLAS.
I HOPE THIS BOOK WILL HELP YOU CONTINUE
OUR FAMILY TRADITIONS OF GREAT LOUISIANA COOKING.

# CONTENTS

# Introduction

I grew up on the back roads and bayous of southwest Louisiana, a place that I did not fully appreciate until later in life. Looking back, I realize that the things I took for granted, like making gumbo with my granny, fishing with my grandad Adams, and family feasts made with produce from the garden, seafood from local waters, and wild game from the woods, were special gifts that have done more to shape who I am as a chef than all my culinary training. As a child every occasion of my life revolved around food—holidays, festivals, funerals, or any other excuse to call the family together. Spicy crawfish boils, crab boils, fish fries, and hearty lakeside breakfasts (pan-fried in a cast-iron skillet) were everyday affairs in my family. Though I eventually struck out on my own, leaving Cajun Country and the food I grew up on behind for a time, those early meals at my grandparents' table would ultimately inspire the menus at Herbsaint and Cochon, my two restaurants in New Orleans.

Today, now happily settled in New Orleans with a family of my own, I have come to recognize the value and importance of this region's culinary heritage. But I've also realized that the food traditions I grew up with are in danger of disappearing, along with the people who created them. Hurricane Katrina was a painful reminder that my region's traditions—the characters, the culture, and the food—are vulnerable. I can't turn back the clock or bring my grandparents back, but because I grew up cooking their food, and because I paid close attention all those years, I am lucky enough to have the recipes and the stories to commemorate a very special place.

My family's food was typical of Acadia Parish (a parish is a county to the rest of y'all), which is in the heart of a region called Acadiana, or Cajun Country. This particular region is a swamp-rimmed stretch of I-10 west of the Atchafalaya Basin and east of Lake Charles. Acadiana is a mostly rural swath that runs along the Gulf Coast all the way to Texas. The landscape is incredibly diverse. There are salt marshes and freshwater bayous, brackish coastal bays and endless swamps (populated by 'gators, snakes, and countless birds and other beasts), and plains tilled and dammed for rice fields and crawfish. It's a land where any given gas station sells tasso, andouille, hogshead cheese, and smoked pig stomach.

Acadia Parish was settled by French exiles from Canada (the term *Cajun* actually comes from the word *Cadian*, a shortened form of the French word *Acadien*). The area also attracted Germans (like my ancestors), who brought along their traditions of sausage making and expert butchering. People in this area are also fondly referred to as "coonasses." That word applies if your family has been in the area a while—regardless of whether you're of French descent or not. The people here love to *pass a good time*, as they say. To this day, when I return, which I do as often as I can, I am amazed at the fun-loving nature of the people.

My first memory of Louisiana (my father was in the military, and we spent the first few years of my life overseas) is of sweltering, oppressive heat. We arrived at my father's parents' house in the tiny town of Sulphur, just outside of Lake Charles, in the dark, in the middle of summer. My sister Michelle and I had been asleep, but the sound of car wheels on the oyster-shell driveway at Granny and Paw Paw Link's woke us up. My memory of this moment is so vivid, in fact, that it could have happened yesterday. The steamy, pine-scented air hung over us as a stifling, motionless blanket. The pulsating drone of cicadas and bullfrogs was near deafening; I had never heard anything like it. I started to sweat through my shirt the minute I got out of the car.

That night marked the beginning of my life in Louisiana, my introduction to its exuberant food and culture—and finding out what my family was all about.

The next morning I experienced my first Louisiana food smells: Community Coffee (dark roast, the kind I still drink at home) boiled on the stovetop and pork smothered with onions and garlic. What an amazing smell—pork, onions, and rich gravy simmering slowly for hours. When we finally sat down to eat, I noticed that even the way the aroma of the steamed rice permeated the gravy was amazing. Food fragrances just seemed to linger in the thick Louisiana air.

My two sets of grandparents lived a quarter mile from one another, and we settled about a mile from them. Between my mother and father, I have thirty-four aunts and uncles. That's ten brothers and sisters on Mom's side and seven on Dad's, plus their spouses and an armada of cousins. To keep things fair, we had to go to both grandparents' houses for meals. Between those two families, we did a lot of eating.

The Zaunbrechers and Links, my uncles and cousins, are still farmers, cultivating thousands of acres of rice as well as crawfish, which handily share the land with rice, alternately feeding off the fallow fields and fertilizing them, making the soil richer for grain production. Needless to say, rice was a very important part of my childhood.

My granny Link moved to Sulphur from Crowley, where her parents had settled in the late 1880s, after emigrating from Germany. Granny's parents were rice farmers, so her food was born of rice married with the Cajun cooking typical of the area: deeply flavored bowls of gumbo, beef pot roasts, and pork roasts smothered with plenty of thinly sliced onions and garlic and served *au jus* (in its natural juices) over rice. It seems like there was always a pot of rice cooking in Granny's house. To this day, when I smell rice cooking I feel as if I'm standing in her kitchen.

Just as the smell of rice will always remind me of Granny Link, the rich, earthy fragrance of pork fat simmering with collard greens transports me to Grandad and Grandma Adams' house. Their kitchen and dining room were tiny, but somehow we always managed to pack twenty-five or more people around the table. Grandad ruled the range in this house, and he cooked Southern fare at its simplest and best. The sheer bounty was always overwhelming. What amazed me was how many different things he produced at a single meal. We might have some smothered greens with ham hocks, cornbread, creamy lima beans simmered with bacon, fried eggplant, creamed corn, duck stew, and the list goes on. The memory of the aroma of all that food cooking in such a small space is a powerful one.


This kind of cooking may or may not sound familiar to you, so before we go any further let's get one thing straight: The overly spiced and blackened food that gained popularity in the 1970s is nothing like the authentic Cajun food that I grew up with. *Real Cajun food* translates to the best ingredients of the area, simply prepared. The flavors are focused and the food is highly seasoned, though not necessarily spicy. Examples include rice (steamed or dirty), roasted meats (served in their own fragrant juices), cured pork and sausage (grilled or used as a seasoning and braised with beans and/or vegetables), oysters (typically fried or baked in dressings), pan-fried fish from local waters, wild game, turtles, crawfish, and lots of shrimp that might be grilled, boiled with spices, or simmered in one-pot meals like fricassees, gumbos, or rich, buttery étouffées. By contrast, *Creole cuisine* is a melting pot of European influences and African and West Indian ingredients. It's considered fancier restaurant fare; you don't see Cajun food on white tablecloths.

Cajun food has come to mean different things to different people, but as far as I'm concerned it's really a very simple concept: Acadiana is populated by farmers who live off the land, and the cuisine is born of this specific location. My second cousin JW, who farms more than 2,000 acres of rice, raises his own food supply, including hogs, chickens, ducks, and pheasants. It seems as though everyone in the area has some sort of homemade smoker, outdoor cooking apparatus, and access to amazing local ingredients. At my cousin Bubba Frey's store in Mowata, you can still go around back and find cages of guinea hens, turtles, squab, and doves right alongside the garden where he grows tomatoes, peppers, and herbs, as well as a gigantic fig tree and the huge smoker where he smokes countless varieties of meat and sausage.

I got my first paying job in an Iranian-owned Mexican restaurant when I was fifteen. I started out washing dishes, and, man, that was hard work! Finally, the older guys in their midtwenties (they bought me my first bottle of rum) taught me how to work the line. It went something like this: *Here's the plate, you put the tortilla here, a spoon of this there, then this sauce and cheese, then into the oven, and there you go.*

I was attending Louisiana State University and working at Sammy's Bar and Grill in Baton Rouge when I met my wife, Amanda Hammack. I was five years into a finance major and at the end of my rope. I wasn't sure what I wanted to do, but I knew I wanted more than the small-town life of my childhood. I wanted to be different, to redefine myself, and I was desperate to get out of Louisiana. Amanda felt the same way, and two months later we moved to northern California.

When we arrived in San Francisco, I needed an income fast. I got a job at a breakfast dive in the lower Haight popular with aspiring rock stars, tattooed bikers, and junkies. For a twenty-three-year-old straight out of Louisiana, the scene was intimidating, but looking into the dining room at all the strange and different people, and the frenetic, exciting scene, I had a revelation: I *loved* cooking, and I wanted to do it forever.

The years that followed included stints at some of San Francisco's top restaurants, as well as a degree from the California Culinary Academy. In 1995, Amanda was accepted at Tulane, and we returned to New Orleans, where I got a job at Bayona, Susan Spicer's widely respected restaurant in the French Quarter. After Amanda graduated, we returned to San Francisco for one more West Coast adventure before relocating to Louisiana, this time for good, in 1999.

That was the year our daughter Cassidy was born, and my perspective on a lot of things changed. The word *family* took on new meaning, and for the first time I had to be responsible for someone other than myself. Amanda and I wanted to buy a house, and I knew I wanted to open my own restaurant—a bistro that would meld the fresh, ingredient-driven food that I'd come to love in California with the deepest Louisiana flavors. I brainstormed with Susan Spicer, who was also looking to open a bistro-style restaurant. We joined forces with partner Ken Jackson and my in-laws, Bill Hammack and Janice Parmelee. We found a sunny space in the warehouse district, on a corner of St. Charles with a streetcar running past out front, and Herbsaint was born. We opened the doors in October 2000, and we hit the ground running. I'm proud to say the restaurant has been a roaring success ever since.

Herbsaint is named after a locally made anise-flavored liqueur, but its roots are in Acadia Parish. The menu is a sort of modern Creole: seafood from local waters and hearty meat and pork dishes, along with the game and sausages of Cajun cuisine, crossed with classical French and Italian influences. Susan and I collaborated on the inaugural menu, and after that she was gracious enough to let me to do my own thing.

Proud as I was of the menu at Herbsaint, I felt strongly that authentic Cajun and *home-style* Southern cooking were seriously underrepresented in our city. Increasingly interested in the rustic foods I'd grown up with, I started ordering whole pigs and breaking them down. I got excited about making my own boudin sausage and house-cured bacon. It dawned on me that I had the inspiration, and the kitchen talent, to do another restaurant. I partnered with Stephen Stryjewski, and the concept for Cochon (French for "pig"), a restaurant that would celebrate authentic Cajun, was born.

Then Hurricane Katrina blew through town and changed just about everything.

Amanda and I lost our house and all of our possessions in the storm and we had to relocate. Herbsaint was closed for several weeks, and Cochon's opening was delayed for several months. The storm was a painful reminder that nothing can be taken for granted.

When Katrina forced us to evacuate the city, we stayed with my dad in Lake Charles. The period of exile that followed led to some powerful emotions and real-izations. For the first time, I was spending all day in the kitchen, cooking for my extended family just as my grandparents used to do. Watching me make the gumbo, my sister said how much I looked like Grandad Adams (talking to myself and all), and I relished the comparison. I knew that the food of my region at the new restaurant was simply the right thing to do.

With Cochon's unabashedly home-style menu, its commitment to local products, the in-house *boucherie* (butcher shop), and the photos of my family on the walls, I have really come full circle. We serve boudin balls, crawfish pies, eggplant with shrimp dressing, and rabbit stew topped with dumplings. Desserts like blueberry cobbler and German chocolate cake are equally rustic.

The emotional confluence of the past years—Hurricane Katrina, my consequent decision to commit to New Orleans, the success of Cochon, and the birth of my son Nico—made my desire even stronger to document a time when food *mattered.*

It took me a while to figure out just how lucky I was to have been able to enjoy the food my grandparents dished up with such ease. Like most kids, I assumed that everyone ate as we did. But to this day I have not experienced home cooking that can come close. The recipes and the stories that follow are my tribute to this unsur-passed slice of rustic, unpretentious fare—what I call *Real Cajun.* Here's hoping you, too, will pass a good time reading and cooking from these pages.

# Notes on Cooking

Real Cajun food is *rustic*; it does not require a lot of fancy ingredients or the latest gadgets. My grandparents' food relied mostly on inexpensive pantry staples and the bounty of local ingredients (things like fresh produce, sausage, and seafood that are available to most cooks around the country). These recipes are resourceful and economical; shrimp shells and chicken carcasses and vegetable peelings are recycled to make stock, and so forth.

During the cooking process, keep in mind that the actual heat and temperatures conveyed by the numbers on the dial vary greatly, so don't get too attached to cooking and baking times. Instead, pay attention to what's happening in the pot (or oven), and adjust times accordingly.

When it comes to spices and seasonings, I am not terribly finicky about sourcing. Ideally, spices should be fresh, but beyond that don't fret too much. I won't be calling for Turkish oregano or smoked paprika, for instance; the bottle sold at the grocery store simply labeled "paprika" will do just fine.

However, I have developed a few preferences and habits that have become second nature in my cooking. What follows is a guide to staple ingredients used in this book.

**Salt:** Kosher salt is the choice in my restaurants and at home, because I like the clean taste and the feel of the larger crystals between my fingers when I season foods. Kosher salt is also good because you can see it set up on the food before it soaks in, which allows you to see how much you are seasoning, whereas iodized salt disappears.

**Black pepper:** I always use freshly ground.

**Flour:** Use all-purpose.

**Butter:** I prefer unsalted butter for everything.

**Eggs:** I always use those graded large; this is particularly important for baking.

**Peppers and chiles:** These should be stemmed and seeded unless specified otherwise. When deciding what chiles to use, consider the heat balance of the dish. Cajun cooking is more about the flavors of chiles, rather than simple heat. This is one reason bell peppers are so prominent in Cajun food. They have a fresh green flavor and almost no heat. To me, though, they lack punch, so I often use a mixture of poblanos and jalapeños, and even fresh cayenne peppers. I like their fresh chile flavor and moderate heat, and in some dishes I prefer to get heat from fresh chiles rather than chile powders. I combine fresh and dried chiles because they balance each other.

**Bay leaves:** You can use fresh bay leaves for a more pungent flavor, but I mostly use dried. If you use fresh, you will want to use a few less.

**Hot sauce:** Louisiana, Crystal, and Tabasco are my favorite brands.

**Creole mustard:** This grainy mustard has a spicy horseradish flavor, but you can use any whole-grain mustard.

**Paprika:** I generally use hot paprika (as opposed to sweet Hungarian paprika), but the variety is not terribly important. A jar that is not labeled "hot" or "sweet" is just fine.

**Scallions:** I trim both ends of the scallions and use both the white and green parts.

I have adapted the recipes included in this book for home cooks, but feel free to adjust the flavors as you see fit. For instance, I like a lot of salt and spice in my food. Taste the dish as you go, and season to your own preference. Cook to make yourself and your family happy, because that's really what it is all about.

# Donnie's Spice Mix

MAKES SCANT 1 CUP

When I'm at home and want to cook something quick and easy, I love having this blend in my cabinet so I don't have to fish out a bunch of spices. There is no salt in this mix, so be sure to add salt to whatever you are cooking. (I do the salt separately because some food needs more of it than others.) I use this mix for everything from fish fillets to jambalaya.

For the record, I let a few people call me Donnie—my cousin Billy Boy, Richard Reddington, Grandma Hammack, and my coauthor, Paula. It was the latter who named this recipe.

2 tablespoons cayenne pepper
2 tablespoons paprika
1 tablespoon ground white pepper
1 tablespoon ground black pepper
4 tablespoons chili powder
1 tablespoon garlic powder

Combine spices in a small bowl and store in a cool, dark place in a tightly sealed container.

LA VIE COCHON

My most cherished, most powerful food memories involve two ingredients: rice and pork. They're both crucial to Cajun cooking, and while I can't imagine one without the other, no single food embodies the spirit and culture of southwest Louisiana better than the mighty pig. Pork is a snack ("Pass the spiced cracklings and boudin balls"), a seasoning (as in bacon simmered with green beans or smoked sausage in a stew), and quite often the centerpiece of a meal. It's no wonder that the restaurant I devoted to authentic Cajun cooking is known by the French word for "pig."

When I drive home to Lake Charles from New Orleans I cross what's known as the Atchafalaya swamp by means of a twenty-two-mile bridge between Baton Rouge and Lafayette. Henderson, Louisiana, is the official start of Cajun Country. My first order of business at this point is to get some boudin—a sausage made from pork and rice—and a cold beer or two. Once I've had a taste of both, I'm home.

You can actually trace the importance of pork and rice through my family tree. My great-great-grandfather Nicholas Zaunbrecher (my son Nico's namesake) immigrated to Rayne, Louisiana, along with forty other families from Geilenkirchen, Germany, in 1881, and they settled in a community called Robert's Cove. He is credited with being the first person to ship rice to New Orleans, which started Louisiana's commercial rice industry. He also devised several irrigation methods that enabled the industry to thrive. Nicholas went on to marry and have eleven children, including a son, Lorenz. When Lorenz died, he had eighty-eight grandchildren, one of them being my father, Gene.

Along with farming, the Zaunbrechers brought a tradition of sausage making to southwest Louisiana, with family recipes that are still being used today.

Every Tuesday night at the Zaunbrecher "camp" (the local term for the family homestead), where the sausage is made, my relatives get together and take turns cooking. You won't find any stereotypically spicy food here; instead, you'll find wonderful meats "smothered" or simmered in sauces made from their natural juices, boudin, smoked sausage, buttery homemade yeast rolls, garden-fresh cucumber and tomato salads, and, of course, plenty of hot steamed rice. In Cajun Country, every meal is served with rice. These meals are a testament to my family's history and culture, and are examples of real home-style Cajun cooking.

The recipes in this chapter showcase the pig in all its guises. I've included recipes for homemade bacon and tasso, two ingredients that are the backbone of much of my cooking. There are also simple pork mixtures you can pat out as patties for breakfast, smoked sausages from my family's recipe boxes; moist, flavorful boudin—my favorite food in the whole world—and a few contemporary dishes like Braised Sausage with Chiles that I love to prepare at home for easy weeknight dinners. Each in its own way celebrates *La vie cochon*.

# Homemade Bacon

MAKES ABOUT 4 POUNDS

I don't know how many different types of bacon I have eaten and cooked in my career, but trust me, it's been a lot. For years I was on a quest for the *best bacon around*. I would not advise you to try this at home. Although I never met a strip of bacon that I didn't like, some are definitely better than others.

There are several things that give bacon its unique taste and character. The first and most important factor is the quality of pork. Mass-produced factory-farmed pork does not have much flavor. Fortunately, there are a growing number of smaller producers who raise meat naturally or organically, sometimes relying on heirloom breeds, and their pigs have by far the best taste. (For some of my favorite producers, see Resources [page 250].) The second consideration is the amount of fat. I look for a nice ratio of fat and meat, with a bent toward the fattier side. Other considerations are salt, sugar, and smoke—too much or too little of any of those can ruin a dish.

After years of buying bacon for my restaurants, we decided to start making our own and found out just how easy it is. It's also a much better bacon than any I've ever had (and a third of the price). I always keep a slab in my freezer at home so it's there whenever the mood strikes me.

For the best results, slice the bacon when it is cold (room-temperature bacon is too soft and flabby to slice). Slice the bacon as thin or thick as you like. I like the chewy texture (and meaty bite) of thick, slightly undercooked slices that showcase the flavor of the pork. Thinner slices will cook up crisper.

| | |
|---|---|
| 4 pounds fresh boneless pork belly, cut into 1-pound pieces | 3¼ cups granulated sugar |
| 4 cups kosher salt | ¾ cup brown sugar, packed |
| | ¾ teaspoon curing salt (see Sidebar) |

Pat the pork belly with paper towels to remove excess moisture.

Combine the salt, sugar, brown sugar, and curing salt in a mixing bowl. Place the pork in a baking pan or a large plastic container; cover the top of the pork with a layer of the salt mixture, then flip it over and bury the meat in the remaining mixture. Refrigerate the pork, covered, for 10 days. This will "cure" the belly, and you will have what's known as salt pork or unsmoked bacon.

Remove the pork from the salt and rinse under cold water; pat dry with paper towels. Place the pork on a glazing rack (or on cake racks set on baking sheets) and refrigerate overnight to air-dry.

Smoke the pork at about 140°F for about 1 hour. The bacon can now can be held in the refrigerator or frozen.

## CURING SALT

Curing salt typically contains sugar, nitrates, and curing agents that help preserve meat longer; it keeps the inside of the meat an appealing pink color (without it the meat would turn gray). Regular salt cannot be used as a substitute.

# Pork Belly Cracklins

SERVES 6 TO 8 FAT LOVERS AS A SNACK

In moderation, cracklins, or cubes of deep-fried pork fat that are typically salted and spiced, are one of the best snacks around. Cracklins fall into the boudin food group, meaning they are an "any time, anywhere" food in Cajun Country. They are my preferred snack on a road trip.

Traditionally, cracklins are made from a pig's back fat (my favorite kind, especially if you can buy them super-fresh). The skin cracks when fried, leaving a juicy pocket of pork fat underneath that squirts in your mouth when you bite into it. But these days cracklins are mostly made from the pork belly, which is actually more flavorful (and a bit less fatty) because they still have a big fatty chunk of meat attached under the skin.

To cook cracklins I prefer the classic method used to make French fries: The cracklins are first blanched in hot oil, then deep-fried a second time at a higher temperature so they're lighter and crispier. Depending on the size of the cracklins, they may need a little more or less cooking time than indicated below. Basically you want to cook them until they're golden brown and the skin bubbles up and cracks—this should only take a few minutes on the second frying.

Cracklins are best served in small brown paper bags, but they're also great on top of grits, pork roasts, and stirred into cornbread batter. They're best eaten the same day that they're fried, but they will keep one day, stored at room temperature in an airtight container.

| | |
|---|---|
| 2 pounds pork belly with skin | 2 teaspoons kosher salt |
| 1 gallon peanut oil | 2 teaspoons Donnie's Spice Mix (page 15) |

Cut the belly pieces into 1½-inch squares, leaving the skin on.

Heat the oil over medium-high heat in a deep, heavy-bottomed pot. Make sure the pot you use is very deep—you want 6 to 10 inches from the top of the oil to the rim of the pan. Place a deep-frying thermometer on the pot.

When the oil reaches 225°F, add the pork cubes and cook, stirring gently (especially at the beginning, so they don't clump together), for 15 to 20 minutes, until light golden brown.

Using a sieve, transfer the cracklins to a plate lined with paper towels and cool for at least 20 minutes.

After the cracklins have cooled, reheat the oil to 400° to 425°F. Add the cracklins and cook for another 3 to 5 minutes, until the skin "cracks" or bubbles up.

Transfer the cracklins to a plate lined with fresh paper towels and cool for a minute, then immediately toss them into a mixing bowl and toss with the salt and spice.

# Cajun Tasso

MAKES ABOUT 5 POUNDS

Simply put, tasso is Cajun ham. The fattier parts of the pig find their way into sausage, but tasso is usually made with the leaner cuts—and in Cajun Country, even pork butt is considered a leaner cut. Tasso is mainly used as a flavoring for soups, gumbos, and jambalaya; I always use it in my duck or rabbit gumbo. It's also especially good in cream-based sauces, such as Spicy Crawfish Fettuccine (page 58).

For this recipe I use a brine to keep the pork moist during smoking; a standard pork brine that I also use for chops or ham. Allspice, juniper, and star anise are not traditional in Cajun cooking, but I love the way they infuse the meat with flavor. The rub is not extremely spicy, but it still packs a little punch. If you prefer yours spicier, just up the cayenne.

Brine
1½ gallons water
¾ cup sugar
¾ cup kosher salt
5 garlic cloves
2 tablespoons allspice berries
2 tablespoons juniper berries
5 star anise pods
4 tablespoons black peppercorns
½ teaspoon curing salt (see Sidebar, page 21)
1 bunch fresh thyme
1 bunch fresh sage leaves

7–8 pound boneless pork butt, cut into 5 by 2-inch slices

Tasso spice
1½ cups paprika
½ cup chili powder
3 tablespoons cayenne pepper
2 tablespoons ground white pepper
2 tablespoons red pepper flakes (see Note)
¼ cup plus 2 tablespoons table salt
¼ cup dried oregano
2 tablespoons garlic powder

Combine the brine ingredients in a large pot and bring to a boil over high heat, then cool to room temperature. (To cool the brine quickly, set the pot into a large bowl or sink full of ice water.)

When the brine has cooled, transfer it to an extra-large resealable plastic bag or a large bowl. Add the pork and seal the bag or cover the bowl, making sure the pork is submerged. Refrigerate for 2 days.

Remove the pork slices from the brine and pat dry with paper towels. Stir together the tasso spices in a large bowl. Add the pork and toss until the meat is evenly coated. Put the seasoned pork pieces on a glazing (or cake) rack and let them air-dry at room temperature for 1 day.

Smoke at 220°F for about 1 hour, until the tasso is firm to the touch and the inside temperature is 160°F. (For a drier or more traditional tasso, coat the meat with spices and cure on a rack in a refrigerator for 3 days.)

NOTE: I usually seek out seedless red pepper flakes at Asian markets. I like them without the seeds because they are not as spicy, so I can use more of them and get a better chile flavor without all the heat.

# Simple Pork Sausage

MAKES ABOUT 6 POUNDS

This simple "green" sausage (that is, uncooked and unsmoked) is for making Bolognese sauce, soups, or simply to grill.

Meat grinders and sausage stuffers are available at most good food-supply stores, and they are easy to use. If you own a Kitchen-Aid stand mixer, the sausage attachment works just fine. If you don't feel like making that commitment, form this sausage into patties for burgers or breakfast. It is also great in pastas with tomato- and cream-based sauces.

6 pounds boneless pork butt
1½ pounds pork fat back
4 tablespoons kosher salt
1 tablespoon sugar
2 teaspoons ground fennel
1 teaspoon ground white pepper
2 teaspoons cayenne pepper

2 teaspoons paprika
2 teaspoons red pepper flakes
2 teaspoons ground black pepper
1 tablespoon dried oregano
3 tablespoons Worcestershire sauce
1 tablespoon minced garlic
6 to 8 feet of sausage casings, rinsed

Cut the pork and fat back into 2-inch squares. Whisk together the salt, sugar, spices, Worcestershire, and garlic in a large bowl, add the pork and fat, and toss until evenly coated. Refrigerate the meat, covered, overnight.

Using a mixer fitted with a grinding attachment, grind the pork mixture into the casings (see Sidebar, page 28), twisting the casing into links of the desired lengths. This sausage can then be gently poached in water or beer, grilled, or smoked.

NOTE: To create sausage with a finer, more emulsified texture (think hot dogs), puree half the ground sausage in a food processor, then pass the finely ground meat through the grinder a second time, with the remaining meat.

## STUFFING CASINGS

To stuff sausage into casings, slide the appropriate
length of the rinsed casings onto the feeder nozzle.
Tie a knot on the opposite end of the casing before
you begin extruding the meat. Guide the sausage
onto a baking sheet that has been moistened with a
small amount of water to keep the casings from
drying out. Twist the sausage into the desired
lengths.

In Louisiana, sausage casings are generally sold
in "hanks," which should be enough for 100 pounds
of sausage. They come packed in salt, so they last a
long time. You might try to buy them from a local
butcher or grocery store that makes their own
sausages. If your sausage endeavors will be on a
smaller scale, you can usually find smaller packages
of casings in the meat section at most
supermarkets.

A 6-inch link of sausage weighs about 6 ounces.
Ten pounds of meat should yield about 26 links. You
should count on 8 inches of casing per 6-inch link,
so for 10 pounds you would need about 12 feet of
casings.

# My Boudin

MAKES 4 POUNDS

Boudin, the king of Cajun food, is my favorite thing in the world to eat. It is a unique food in that it can be breakfast, lunch, dinner, a snack, or car food. Whereas most of the country might show up at a morning get-together with donuts, we show up with boudin. And no two boudins are exactly alike—that's amazing, considering they all have basically the same ingredients of rice and pork.

One of the best boudins I've had is made by my cousin Bubba Frey, who owns the Mowata General Store in the heart of the German settlement between the Link and Zaunbrecher rice fields, but all my cousins down there make their own boudin. One cousin told me that meat from the temple of the pig's head makes the best boudin, while another claims that a combination of hog jowl and shoulder meat is the secret. The truth is, they are *all* good.

This recipe combines elements from all of the different boudins I've eaten in my day. There's liver in it but just enough, it's nicely spiced but won't burn your mouth, and it has the perfect amount of rice.

2 pounds boneless pork shoulder, cut into 1-inch cubes
½ pound pork liver, cut into 1-inch cubes
1 small onion, chopped
2 celery stalks, chopped
1 medium poblano chile, stemmed, seeded, and chopped
3 medium jalapeño peppers, stemmed, seeded, and chopped
6 garlic cloves, coarsely chopped
4 tablespoons kosher salt
1 tablespoon ground black pepper

1 tablespoon ground white pepper
½ teaspoon curing salt (see Sidebar, page 21)
1 teaspoon cayenne pepper
1 teaspoon chili powder
7 cups cooked white rice
1 cup chopped fresh parsley
1 cup chopped scallions (green and white parts)
4 to 6 feet of sausage casings (optional), rinsed

Combine the pork, liver, vegetables, and seasonings in a bowl and marinate for 1 hour or overnight, covered, in the refrigerator. Place the marinated mixture in a large pot and cover the meat with water (by 1 to 2 inches). Bring the mixture to a boil, reduce the heat, and simmer until the meat is tender, about 1 hour and 45 minutes.

Remove the pot from the heat and strain, reserving the liquid. Allow the mixture to cool slightly, then put the solids through a meat grinder set on coarse grind. (You can also chop with a knife if you don't have a meat grinder, which is what I usually do anyway.)

Place the ground meat in a large bowl. Using a wooden spoon or rubber spatula, mix in the cooked rice, parsley, scallions, and the reserved cooking liquid. Stir vigorously for 5 minutes. When the boudin-rice mixture is first combined, it looks very wet and it's pretty spicy. Don't worry; after poaching, the rice absorbs the excess moisture and much of the spice. The wet texture and extra spice ensure that your final boudin will be moist and full of flavor.

At this point you can feed the sausage into the casings (see Sidebar, page 28). Poach the links gently in hot (not bubbling) water for about 10 minutes, then serve. Alternatively, you can use the mixture as a stuffing for chicken, or roll it into "boudin balls," dredge in bread crumbs, and fry in hot oil until golden brown.

NOTE: To eat fresh, hot poached boudin, bite into the link and use your teeth and fingers to gently pull the meat out of its soft casing. (The casings are only eaten when the boudin is grilled or smoked and they become crisp.) You can also slice the boudin and tease the meat out with a fork, though utensils are not encouraged.

Some locals eat boudin with a dab of Creole mustard, a drizzle of cane syrup, a French roll, or a few crackers. But most feel that it, like a few of life's other illicit pleasures, is best enjoyed in the heat of the moment, eaten straight from the wrapper, while sitting in one's car. This is not a region known for its pretension: It is fondly said that a Cajun seven-course meal is a pound of boudin and a six-pack of beer.

# Zaunbrecher Deer Sausage

MAKES ABOUT 5 POUNDS

Sausage is virtually synonymous with pork, but in Louisiana hunting is still an important part of the food-supply chain, and at the end of deer season, it's time for everyone to use the venison they have accumulated.

The recipe I've included here is similar to the Zaunbrechers', a 60:40 mix of deer and pork. Venison adds a dense meaty taste to sausage; the fatty pork contributes wonderful flavor and much-needed moisture. As the story goes, my great-great-grandfather Nicholas brought this recipe with him from Germany. The recipe has been changed slightly over the years (it used to contain nutmeg, for instance), but the heart of the seasoning remains the same.

When I participated in my first Zaunbrecher sausage fest, I assumed that we might make a hundred pounds, but we made 2,000 pounds of deer sausage that day. This recipe yields 5 pounds of sausage, but it can easily be doubled. When making sausage, keep both the meat and your grinding equipment very cold; that makes it easier to grind the meat. This is not a very spicy sausage. If you like it hotter, add another teaspoon of cayenne and black pepper or a teaspoon of red pepper flakes.

3 pounds boneless pork butt
2 pounds boneless deer meat (see Note)
3 tablespoons kosher salt
2 teaspoons ground black pepper
2 teaspoons cayenne pepper
1 teaspoon ground white pepper

¼ teaspoon curing salt (see Sidebar, page 21)
1⅓ tablespoons sugar
¾ teaspoon garlic powder
1 cup water
About 6 feet of sausage casings, rinsed

Cut the pork and venison into 2-inch squares.

In a mixing bowl, combine all the spices, add the water, and stir well. Add the meat and, using your hands, toss well until evenly coated with the spice mixture. Using a mixer fitted with a grinding attachment, grind the meat, then attach about 6 feet of casing and stuff into desired lengths (see Sidebar, page 28).

Smoke at 80°-100°F for about 4 hours. At this point, the sausages will not be fully cooked. Store them in the refrigerator and finish cooking before serving.

NOTE: The loins and saddles of deer are typically grilled, smoked, or fried. You'll want to use the legs and other fattier cuts for making sausage.

## CAJUN SAUSAGE

As any Cajun will tell you, there are many different ways to make sausage. Throughout Acadiana, recipes vary as to whether or not to add curing salt, MSG, garlic, or even liver. Curing salt is essential for smoked sausage, however. My cousin told me that one time when he made sausage he accidentally left the curing salt out and when he smoked it, the mixture went sour. Apparently the low to moderate heat and slow smoking process means the meat is susceptible to spoilage, but the curing salt helps prevent that. Curing salt also gives meat an appealing pink color and adds saltiness. But if you're making green (unsmoked) sausage, there's no need for curing salt. As far as MSG is concerned, I like the increased flavor it provides, but as MSG can cause adverse reactions in some people I leave it out.

# Smothered Pork Roast over Rice

SERVES 8 TO 10

Whenever we drove into Granny's driveway, we would know when she was cooking this dish because its rich aroma would hit us as soon as we stepped out of the car.

This roast embodies the simple, not necessarily spicy, style of Cajun cooking (notice there is no cayenne). The stewing method for cooking meat is also used in several other Cajun dishes calling for venison, duck, rabbit, and chicken. Technically the preparation is an *étouffée*, which means "smothered," but everyone in these parts favors the Southern term when used for larger cuts of meat swimming in onions and sauce.

1 (6- to 7-pound) boneless pork roast (shoulder or butt)
Kosher salt
Ground black pepper
2 large onions, thinly sliced
8 garlic cloves, thinly sliced
3 tablespoons fresh thyme leaves
1 tablespoon dried rosemary, crumbled

2 tablespoons vegetable oil
8 tablespoons (1 stick) butter
½ cup all-purpose flour
4 cups chicken broth
Juice of ½ lemon (optional)
Perfect Steamed Rice (recipe follows)

Preheat the oven to 275°F.

Season the pork very generously with salt and pepper, rubbing the seasonings into the fat and flesh of the meat. Set the roast aside for at least 30 minutes or up to 1 hour at room temperature.

Combine the onions, garlic, thyme, and rosemary in a medium mixing bowl and toss to combine.

Heat the vegetable oil in a Dutch oven over medium-high heat. When the oil is very hot, sear the meat on all sides until deeply browned and crusty, 10 to 12 minutes total.

Transfer the meat to a plate, reduce the heat to medium, and then stir in the butter. When the butter has melted, stir in the flour to make a roux and continue to cook, stirring, until the roux turns a dark peanut butter color, about 10 minutes.

Add the onion mixture and cook, stirring, until all the ingredients are well coated and the mixture is thick. Whisk in the chicken broth and bring to a simmer, stirring constantly. Return the pork to the Dutch oven, spoon some of the onion mixture over the meat, cover, and roast for about 3 hours, turning and basting the pork every 30 minutes or so, until the meat will break apart when pressed gently with a fork.

At this point, you can serve the roast right out of the pan, or transfer it to a plate, then simmer the pan drippings, skimming off excess fat, until reduced by about one-third, or until it coats the back of a spoon. Add the lemon juice and taste for seasonings.

Before serving, sprinkle the roast with some additional salt. Serve the roast smothered with a generous amount of sauce and hot steamed rice.

# Perfect Steamed Rice

MAKES 3 CUPS

I have never been in a kitchen in southern Louisiana that doesn't have a rice cooker. You are as sure to see one on the counter as you are to find the trash under the sink. There are countless ways to cook rice, and various cultures have their own methods. In Cajun Country, rice is almost always steamed. Some people like their rice somewhat sticky, because it soaks up rich and fragrant sauces better, while others like the individual rice grains to be a bit drier and separate. If you fall into the latter category, rinse the rice in cold water before cooking. (Another method for keeping rice grains separate is to cook them pilaf style by sautéing the rice briefly in butter or oil—and often minced onions—before adding the cooking liquid; the fat coats the grains and helps them remain separate during cooking.)

I generally like my rice steamed (and sticky) because steaming brings out its natural nutty flavor and aroma. The fragrance of steamed rice always reminds me of where I came from, and it makes me anticipate whatever it is I'm serving with the rice. This recipe can be doubled or tripled as needed, as long as the ratio of 1 part rice to 1½ parts water remains the same.

1 cup long-grain rice
1½ cups water
2 bay leaves
Pinch of salt

Combine the rice, water, bay leaves, and salt in a medium saucepan and bring to a boil over medium-high heat. Reduce the heat to very low, cover with a tight-fitting lid, and simmer for 15-20 minutes. Remove from the heat, and keep covered for an additional 5 minutes. Remove the lid, cool for a few minutes, and then fluff the rice with a fork.

# Smoked Sausage and Lima Bean Stew

SERVES 4

Unlike recipes made with dried beans, this preparation calls for fresh lima beans, though any fresh shell bean can be used with similar effect. Fresh beans don't take nearly as long to cook, and they impart a summery flavor that you won't get from dried beans.

This stew is great served over hot steamed rice but is also really delicious on its own. If you're not serving it over rice, consider adding 1 cup of diced potatoes along with the other vegetables.

2 tablespoons olive oil
6 ounces mild smoked sausage (your
    favorite variety), cut into ¾-inch cubes
1 small onion, thinly sliced
1 celery stalk, diced
1 small carrot, diced

1 medium turnip, diced
½ teaspoon salt
¼ teaspoon ground black pepper
4 cups water or chicken stock
2 cups shelled fresh (or frozen) lima beans
    (about 1¼ pounds in the shell)

Heat the oil in a large Dutch oven or pot over medium-high heat. Add the sausage and cook, stirring, for 2 minutes, until lightly browned, then add the onion, celery, carrot, turnip, salt, and pepper and cook for another 5 minutes, until the vegetables are tender. Add the water and bring to a boil, then reduce the heat and simmer for 15 minutes. Add the lima beans and simmer for another 15 minutes, until the lima beans are tender. Taste the stew and adjust seasonings as desired.

# Italian-Style Roast Pork Shoulder

SERVES 10 TO 12

Sometimes in the South it's just too hot to eat a smothered, braised, falling-apart pork roast. This is a "lighter" version of roast pork. On a recent trip to Tuscany I came across a farmer's market where one of the vendors was selling *porchetta*, a whole boned rotisserie-roasted pig. It was amazingly flavorful, tender, garlicky, and my favorite, salty.

Since boning a whole pig takes considerable knife skills, I've based this recipe on a pork butt or boned leg. The important part is the seasoning—in other words, lots of salt and garlic. It's really amazing how much salt pork can take and how much it adds to the roast.

One of my favorite snacks is sliced pork on Linda Zaunbrecher's Homemade Rolls (page 168) with some garlic mayonnaise and pickled cabbage. Cook this roast to medium so that it still has some pink in the middle, and stays tender and juicy, and slice only what you plan to serve.

1 (7-pound) boneless pork butt

Inside Seasonings
3 tablespoons kosher salt
1 teaspoon ground black pepper
1 tablespoon ground fennel
2 tablespoons minced garlic
1 tablespoon chopped fresh thyme or
   rosemary

Outside Seasonings
2 tablespoons kosher salt
1 teaspoon ground black pepper

4 tablespoons vegetable oil
1 large onion, cut into ½-inch slices

Make a vertical cut down the center of the pork, cutting only halfway through, then turn knife 90° degrees to the right and cut halfway through. Do the same on the other side of the center cut. (This technique is called butterflying.) This will open up the pork into a flat slab to allow you to season it well.

Using your hands, smear the seasoning all over the meat. I usually make a few small cuts inside the meat, about 1-inch deep, so that I can really get the seasonings worked in. Fold the pork back up and truss with kitchen twine. Coat the outside of the roast with salt and pepper.

Preheat the oven to 325°F.

Heat the vegetable oil in a Dutch oven or roasting pan over medium-high heat. Add the roast and sear on all sides until crusty and brown all over.

Arrange the sliced onion in a roasting pan and set the roast on top. Roast for 1½ to 2 hours, until the pork reaches an internal temperature of 145° to 155°F. Allow the roast to rest for at least 30 minutes before slicing.

# Braised Sausage with Chiles

SERVES 4

Many recipes call for sausage as a flavor enhancer, but in this recipe it's the star. As much as I love Southern dishes smothered in brown gravy, this recipe is a different type of "smothered." The sweetness of peppers and the acidity of vinegar and mustard are great complements to the richness of the sausage. At Cochon, we serve a similar version of this dish over creamy grits enriched with Creole cream cheese (an extra thick, tart variety of cream cheese available in New Orleans; sour cream or crème fraîche are fine as substitutes).

1 tablespoon canola oil
4 (4-ounce) pork sausage links
1 (12-ounce) bottle amber beer
¼ cup red wine vinegar
½ medium onion, thinly sliced
1 small red bell pepper, cored, seeded, and julienned
1 jalapeño pepper, stemmed, seeded, and thinly sliced

2 garlic cloves, finely chopped
2 tablespoons Creole (or whole-grain) mustard
4 rosemary sprigs
1 teaspoon salt
Perfect Steamed Rice (page 36), for serving

Heat the canola oil in a large skillet over medium-high heat. Add the sausage and sear for 5 minutes, turning as necessary until evenly browned.

Add the beer and vinegar and cook for 1 minute, until slightly reduced. Add the onion, red pepper, jalapeño, garlic, mustard, rosemary, and salt and toss well to combine. Reduce the heat to low, cover, and simmer until the peppers are soft, the sausage is cooked through, and the sauce begins to reduce and thicken, 10 to 15 minutes.

Serve over steamed rice, "smothered" with plenty of the sauce.

# Sausage-Stuffed Chicken Thighs

SERVES 4

Thighs have always been my favorite part of a chicken because they have the most flavor and stay moist and delicious. I guess you could consider this dish sort of a roulade, or in French cooking terms, a *ballottine*. After the stuffed thighs are cooked, let them rest on a cutting board for 5 minutes and they will firm up nicely and stay juicy. The sliced rounds make for a great-looking presentation. If you buy thighs individually from the meat case (as opposed to prepackaged varieties), ask for the largest available—they'll be easier to stuff. This recipe is a fun, inexpensive way to prepare a truly great meal, particularly when served with Aunt Sally's Black-Eyed Peas (page 161) or Creamed Sweet Corn (page 151).

8 boneless skin-on chicken thighs
Salt and ground black pepper
5 tablespoons olive oil
8 sage leaves

1 lemon, very thinly sliced
½ pound Simple Pork Sausage (page 27), or other pork sausage

Lay the boneless thighs skin side down on a cutting board and cover with plastic wrap. Evenly pound each piece with the smooth side of a mallet or rolling pin, working from the center of the thigh outward. Transfer the thighs to a baking dish, season with salt and pepper and drizzle with 3 tablespoons of the olive oil (use your fingers to coat each piece evenly). Top each thigh with a sage leaf and a slice of lemon, and marinate in the refrigerator for at least 1 hour, or overnight.

When you're ready to stuff the thighs, discard the lemon and sage and place 1 to 2 tablespoons of sausage in a strip down the middle of each thigh. (Resist the impulse to overload the chicken because you'll want to roll the meat neatly around the filling.) Wrap the chicken snugly around the filling, and secure with two toothpicks.

When you're ready to cook, preheat the oven to 375°F.

Heat the remaining 2 tablespoons olive oil in a cast-iron or nonstick skillet over medium-high heat until very hot but not smoking. Add the chicken skin side down, and sear for 5 to 10 minutes, turning the bundles as necessary to brown on all sides. Transfer the thighs to a baking sheet, then roast in the oven for 15 minutes, until they feel firm when squeezed gently.

Transfer the stuffed thighs to a cutting board or plate to rest, uncovered, for 5 minutes to allow the juices settle. Remove toothpicks, slice each into ½- to 1-inch-thick slices and serve.

FROM LOUISIANA WATERS

When you grow up with something that is abundantly available you tend to take it for granted. It took me years to appreciate fully how amazing the fresh seafood is in Louisiana. Louisiana's fertile coast, rivers, lakes, and bayous are teeming with delicious things to eat: oysters, crabs, redfish, speckled trout, gulf tuna, cobia, crawfish, shrimp, freshwater bass, and bluegills. I've been on saltwater lakes in Louisiana where the shrimp were literally jumping out of the water.

It's no secret that one of our best local products is our sweet fresh shrimp. My dad and I did a lot of shrimping when I was young, in a lot of different spots along the Gulf. To this day I still prefer the taste of the shrimp from the southwestern part of the state, though the shrimp around New Orleans are amazing as well. For me, those that come from waters around Lake Charles have more intense flavor, with just the right amount of salt and sweetness.

When I was a child, little of the seafood we ate came from the store. We feasted on what my family or our relatives caught; fishing was a way of life and a family affair that usually included my dad, mom, sister, uncles, and grandparents. For the most part, that tradition is still alive today, though we do supplement our tables with the fresh shrimp that's sold along the roadside. At my restaurants we still get much of our seafood straight from the source, courtesy of our favorite fisherman, Dino Pertuit, who every day delivers fresh shrimp and blue crabs, netted from waters that span from Lake Hermitage to the Gulf of Mexico. Dino has been shrimping all his life, just as his daddy did.

Eating seafood has been a way of life, too. I've always loved the way fried shrimp smell when they're lifted from hot oil and spread on newspaper to cool, as we eagerly awaited the rest of them to cook. So eager, in fact, that we would invariably grab one as soon as it came out of the oil, only to burn ourselves with the hot juices encased in the crisp breading. My mother used shrimp to make rich shrimp Creole and shrimp gumbo. I couldn't wait to see how Grandad would cook the live catfish he brought home in the ice chests. (Usually they'd be rolled in cornmeal and fried in bacon fat.) Then, of course, there were the boils: heaps of spicy boiled shrimp, crawfish, and crabs, served with sides of potatoes, corn, and hush puppies and dipped in big bowls of cocktail sauce.

One of my favorite things about fishing is how, when I see the fish come out of the water, I'm already thinking about all the ways I can cook it. From the bubbling baked oysters of New Orleans to the rich stuffed crabs in Lake Charles, you can't go wrong with seafood in southern Louisiana.

# Fried Oyster and Bacon Sandwich

MAKES 1 SANDWICH

When I first conceived of this sandwich—a marriage of two of the best foods in the world—for the menu at Cochon, I didn't intend to do a riff on a BLT, but that's basically what this is. Fried plump oysters release their amazing flavor when you bite into them; plenty of bacon makes this a decadent, satisfying sandwich. I always thought that this combination sounded great, but it tastes even better than it sounds. And this recipe obviously doubles or triples perfectly. For the best flavor, use the ripest, sweetest tomatoes you can find.

½ cup all-purpose flour
½ cup cornmeal
1 teaspoon salt
¼ teaspoon ground black pepper
Peanut or vegetable oil, for frying
6 large raw oysters, shucked

2 slices white bread, toasted
2 teaspoons mayonnaise
5 bacon slices, cooked until crisp and
   drained
½ cup shredded iceberg lettuce
1 tomato, cut into 4 very thin slices

Whisk together the flour, cornmeal, salt, and pepper in a medium mixing bowl. Heat 2 inches of oil in a medium saucepan until it reaches 350°F. Toss the oysters in the seasoned flour, shake off the excess, and fry for 3 to 5 minutes, until lightly golden, then drain on paper towels. Don't overfry them or they will become dried out and a little chewy—you want them to be nice and plump.

To assemble the sandwich, spread the toasted bread with mayonnaise, then build upward on one slice starting with the oysters, then bacon, lettuce, and tomato. Top with remaining slice of bread and serve immediately.

# Baked Oysters
# with Herbsaint Hollandaise

SERVES 4 AS AN APPETIZER

Thanks to their mild briny flavor, Louisiana oysters lend themselves exceptionally well to cooking. When it comes to eating oysters on the half-shell, I love the West Coast varieties, but their strong salty taste can overpower a dish.

Herbsaint liqueur and oysters is a classic flavor pairing, while oysters and bacon are a stunning combination (the smoky taste melds beautifully with the oysters' salty and mineral qualities). Topping these hot, bubbling oysters with a few dashes of hot pepper vinegar perks up the rich sauce.

Cook the oysters just until their edges begin to curl; don't overcook them or they will become dry and rubbery. To avoid burning your mouth, let the hot oysters rest a few minutes before eating. This preparation makes a great appetizer to pass or serve on a platter at parties—I guarantee they'll be gone in a flash.

Rock salt, as needed (to hold oyster shells level while cooking and serving)
12 large oysters
2 strips bacon, cut into 1-inch pieces

Herbsaint Hollandaise
2 egg yolks
12 tablespoons (1½ sticks) butter, melted and warm
1 tablespoon fresh lemon juice
1½ tablespoons Herbsaint or other anise-flavored liqueur
1½ teaspoons salt
¼ teaspoon cayenne pepper

Bread crumb topping
1 cup bread crumbs
3 tablespoons butter, melted
2 tablespoons grated Parmesan cheese
½ teaspoon salt
⅛ teaspoon ground black pepper

Hot pepper vinegar, for garnish (optional)

Cover a baking sheet with a thick layer of rock salt. Use an oyster knife to open the oysters and cut them loose from their shells, discarding the top shells. Arrange the oysters on the rock salt.

Fry the bacon squares in a skillet over medium heat until they are about three-fourths cooked (they should be light brown but still moist), then transfer to a plate

covered with paper towels. (Alternatively, you can cook the bacon on a baking sheet in a 350°F oven.)

Heat a medium pot of water to just below a simmer, then set a metal mixing bowl on top, so that it sits over the water without touching it. Place the egg yolks in the bowl and whisk together, over the heat, until they form thick, glossy ribbons. (When you lift the whisk the yolks will form a "ribbon" as they drip back into the bowl.)

Whisking constantly, slowly add half the warm melted butter, the lemon juice, and Herbsaint, then the remaining butter. (Alternating the ingredients will keep the sauce from getting too tight or too loose, which can cause it to "break.") Season the sauce with salt and cayenne.

In a small bowl, combine the bread crumbs with the melted butter, Parmesan, salt, and pepper.

Preheat the oven to 400°F.

Slip a square of bacon under each raw oyster. Spoon 1 tablespoon of hollandaise over each oyster, then cover the sauce generously with the bread crumbs. Bake until the bread crumbs are light golden brown, 5 to 7 minutes. Allow the oysters to cool slightly before serving. Top with a dash or two of hot pepper vinegar, if desired.

NOTE: This preparation for baked oysters relies on the liquor that inspired the name of my bistro, Herbsaint. Herbsaint has an anise flavor similar to Pernod and Pastis. The late 1800s was a grand time in New Orleans. Herbsaint was aged in wormwood to make absinthe, and writers, artists, and bon vivants reveled in the potent elixir. We named the restaurant Herbsaint as an homage to that indulgent spirit.

# Southern-Fried Shrimp

SERVES 4 TO 6

Both of my parents worked full-time when my sister and I were growing up. Consequently, my mother would often call and tell us to pull some shrimp from the deep freezer and have them peeled by the time she got home. (Because my dad and I used to spend a lot of time shrimping, the deep freezer was *always* full of shrimp.) My sister and I relished the assignment because it meant that we were having fried shrimp for dinner.

Of all the countless ways Louisianans prepare shrimp, I think frying is the most common, and in my mind the best. Don't get me wrong—shrimp are fantastic in stews and gumbos because they lend so much of their flavor to the other ingredients, but the great thing about fried shrimp is that the batter and hot oil seal in the shrimp's sweet flavor. With cold beer, spicy cocktail sauce, and cold coleslaw on the side, you'd be hard-pressed to find a more perfect meal.

I've called for large shrimp in this recipe, but any size will work.

2 dozen large shrimp, peeled
½ teaspoon plus 1½ tablespoons salt
¼ teaspoon plus 1 tablespoon ground black pepper
2 cups all-purpose flour
2 teaspoons cayenne pepper

Peanut oil, for frying
1 cup well-shaken buttermilk
2 teaspoons Creole (or whole-grain) mustard (optional—if you want your shrimp tangier)

Place the shrimp in a medium bowl and season with ½ teaspoon salt and ¼ teaspoon black pepper.

In a separate bowl, whisk together the flour with the remaining salt, pepper, and the cayenne.

Heat 3-4 inches of oil in a large pot until very hot, about 350°F (see Note).

Pour the buttermilk (and mustard, if using) over the seasoned shrimp and combine. Working in batches, use a slotted spoon to remove the shrimp from the buttermilk and transfer to the seasoned flour. Using a separate dry spoon or your fingers, toss to evenly coat. Carefully slip the battered shrimp into the fryer and fry until golden brown and crisp, about 5 minutes; drain on paper towels. (Don't over-crowd the fryer with too many shrimp, as this will lower the temperature of the oil and the shrimp won't crisp up as quickly or nicely as they should.)

Cocktail sauce is such a common condiment in Louisiana that few people follow recipes, and restaurants tend to have the ingredients—not the finished product—on the table, allowing people to mix their own to their desired kick. If you're not accustomed to eyeballing your own, here's a great standard formula: 1 cup ketchup, 3 tablespoons horseradish, 2 tablespoons fresh lemon juice, 2 tablespoons Louisiana hot sauce, and 2 teaspoons Worcestershire sauce.

NOTE: If you're like me, and don't have a thermometer for the frying oil, you can test the oil temperature by throwing in a pinch of flour to see how fast it sizzles. If it sinks and doesn't really sizzle, then the oil is not ready; if it browns too quickly, then the oil is too hot. You need to hear a good, lively sizzle before adding the shrimp. My mother relied on a similar method using a piece of white bread.

# Billy Boy's Crawfish Étouffée

SERVES 6 TO 8

Étouffée is one of the most well-known and best-loved Cajun dishes. Nearly every restaurant in the area serves its own version, and it's prepared quite frequently in homes as well. The tail meat of crawfish typically comes in 1-pound Cryovac bags, and usually even has a simple recipe right on the package. As long as you buy good Louisiana crawfish, you can count on the results being delicious.

My personal—and favorite—recipe for étouffée is quite a bit more time-consuming than most but definitely worth the effort. I begin with crawfish that have been cooked in a traditional boil. The first time I made étouffée this way was the day after a party and we had a good bit of boiled crawfish left over. I wanted to see if I could add more crawfish flavor to a classic dish, and the results were fantastic. By using the orange full-of-flavor fat from the crawfish heads, and leaving the fat on the tails, I was able to create a much richer base. As with most crawfish dishes, this is best when you simmer the tails in the sauce until they break down somewhat and release their sweet flavor.

For the best results, turn this dish into a party of your own. Put on some good Cajun music, get an ice-cold beer, add some good company, and start peeling crawfish.

20 pounds boiled crawfish in the shell, or
    2 pounds crawfish tail meat,
    ⅓ cup head fat, and 1 gallon shells

Crawfish stock
1 tablespoon vegetable oil
1 gallon crawfish shells
3 quarts water
Trimmings and scraps (stems, seeds, ribs, and peels) from onion, peppers, celery, and garlic
5 bay leaves

Étouffée
8 tablespoons (1 stick) butter
1 medium onion, finely chopped
3 celery stalks, finely chopped
1 poblano chile, stemmed, seeded, and finely chopped

1 green bell pepper, cored, seeded, and finely chopped
1 jalapeño pepper, stemmed, seeded, and finely chopped
2 garlic cloves, minced
1 tablespoon plus 1 teaspoon salt
1½ teaspoons paprika
1½ teaspoons ground white pepper
1½ teaspoons ground black pepper
1½ teaspoons dried thyme
1 teaspoon red pepper flakes
1 teaspoon cayenne pepper
4 bay leaves
¼ cup all-purpose flour
Juice of ½ lemon
Perfect Steamed Rice (page 36)
5 scallions, thinly sliced (green and white parts)
¼ cup finely chopped parsley
Hot sauce, as desired

# CRAWFISH FARMING

Each year, from January through June, my cousins in Cajun Country are busy farming crawfish. I've had the pleasure of pulling crawfish straight from the rice fields and heading straight to the pot. As I've learned from my cousin Billy Link, aka Billy Boy (this recipe is named for him because he supplies the world's best crawfish for my boils), the crawfish from Crowley are truly unique. Most crawfish come from the Atchafalaya swamp, where they feed on grass. Crawfish that come from the rice fields in Crowley, where my family farms, feed on rice, so they are fatter and sweeter.

Crawfish farming has become a huge industry for the farmers of southwestern Louisiana, and during the season you can find crawfish boils and crawfish dishes all over the region. The good news for people who don't live here is that peeled crawfish tails are easy to order online (see Resources, page 250) and they freeze well. If you use frozen tails, I recommend that you braise the tails about 5 minutes longer so they will break down a little more. Live crawfish can also be shipped, although they will be more expensive.

If using whole crawfish, peel by removing the head and, with the back of your thumbnail, push the fat inside the head into a small bowl. Peel the crawfish around the meat so that the top of the tail still has some fat attached to it. You need about ⅓ cup of fat and 2 pounds crawfish meat.

Once you have enough fat and shells (you'll need 1 gallon of shells for the stock), throw the rest in the lake, or, as my dad had me do, take it 100 yards into the woods and bury it in a 3-foot-deep hole.

Make the stock. Heat the oil in a large stockpot over medium-high heat. Add the shells and crunch them down with a wooden spoon. Add the water, vegetables scraps, and bay leaves and simmer until reduced by about half, about 1 hour. Strain the stock and discard the solids. Measure 4 cups stock for étouffée and freeze any remaining for another use.

Melt 4 tablespoons of the butter and the head fat in a large skillet over medium-high heat. Add the onion, celery, poblano, bell pepper, jalapeño, garlic, and seasonings and cook, stirring, until softened, 3 to 4 minutes. Add the crawfish meat and the remaining 4 tablespoons butter and cook until the butter has melted.

Sprinkle the mixture with the flour and stir until all ingredients are coated. Stir in the crawfish stock and simmer 15 to 20 minutes, until slightly thickened and they begin to break down and release their sweetness. Stir in the lemon juice and taste for seasonings, adding more salt as desired. Serve over rice, garnished with scallions, parsley, and hot sauce, as desired.

# Spicy Crawfish Fettuccine

SERVES 6 TO 8

When I first met my wife, Amanda, I was working at Sammy's Bar and Grill in Baton Rouge. One night, to impress her, I decided to run a special called Redfish Amanda, a pan-fried fillet of redfish, smothered with crawfish cream sauce. The sauce for this pasta is based on that special.

As with most great Louisiana dishes, this one is pretty rich. The addition of tasso provides lightly smoky undertones. Tasso is a common flavoring ingredient in sauces and gumbos, and it works especially well with cream dishes because it doesn't overpower the cream with heavy smoke and fat, as sausage would. The sauce is all about the sweet flavor of crawfish; if you want a lighter dish, replace half of the cream with a few more chopped tomatoes and ¼ cup water.

3 tablespoons butter
1 small onion, finely chopped
1 small poblano chile, stemmed, seeded, and finely chopped
1 small jalapeño pepper, stemmed, seeded, and finely chopped
3 garlic cloves, minced
3 ounces tasso, finely chopped (⅓ cup)
1 teaspoon salt
¼ teaspoon cayenne pepper
¼ teaspoon paprika

1 teaspoon red pepper flakes
3 dashes of hot sauce
4 medium plum tomatoes, finely chopped
1 pound crawfish tail meat
3 tablespoons all-purpose flour
2 cups heavy cream
1 pound fettuccine
Juice of ½ lemon
4 fresh basil leaves
¼ cup thinly sliced scallions
Freshly grated Parmesan cheese, to taste

Bring a large pot of generously salted water to a boil. Melt 1 tablespoon of the butter in a medium saucepan over medium heat. Add the onion, poblano, jalapeño, garlic, tasso, salt, cayenne, paprika, red pepper flakes, and hot sauce and cook, stirring frequently, until the vegetables are softened but not browned, about 5 minutes.

Add the tomatoes and crawfish, reduce heat to medium-low, and simmer for 10 minutes, until the juices have reduced by half.

Add the remaining 2 tablespoons butter and stir until melted; sprinkle with the flour and stir until combined. Add the cream and simmer over low heat for 10 more minutes while continuing to stir occasionally.

While the sauce simmers, cook the fettuccine according to package directions until al dente; drain well.

Stir the lemon juice, basil leaves, and green onions into the sauce. Spoon a generous amount of sauce onto portions of fettuccine and sprinkle lots of Parmeson on top.

# My Hot Sauce

MAKES ABOUT 1½ CUPS

I started making my own hot sauce at my house in New Orleans, using paprika chiles from our garden. Chiles flourish throughout the summer, so this sauce provides a great way to use them up (and enjoy their sunny flavor all year long). But this sauce is a really fun way to experiment with different types of chiles. I call for my new favorite, criolla sellas, which are a medium-size yellow pepper with lemony overtones. I've also used red and green jalapeños, although the criollas have the most complex flavor. If you want some *really* spicy stuff, use habeneros or bird's-eye chiles.

This sauce will perk up everything from scrambled eggs to burgers, gumbo, or jambalaya.

3 cups chopped criolla sella chiles
(or other hot chile)
1 cup salt
½ cup white vinegar

1 cup cider vinegar
2 bay leaves
3 garlic cloves
¼ cup sugar

Combine the chiles and salt in an airtight container and seal. Set aside at room temperature for 4 days.

Rinse the salt off the chiles and drain. Heat the chiles, vinegars, bay leaves, garlic, and sugar in a medium saucepan over medium heat. Bring the mixture to a boil, reduce the heat to low, and simmer for 10 to 15 minutes.

Allow the mixture to cool, then transfer to a blender and puree until smooth. (Use extreme caution when blending so you don't splatter the sauce anywhere near your eyes.) Store the sauce in the refrigerator, in a tightly sealed sterilized glass jar.

NOTE: When working with chiles be sure to wash your hands really well when you're finished, and be careful not to wipe your brow or eyes. And for the guys, whatever you do, do not go to the restroom without washing your hands first (really important!).

# Vietnamese Marinated Shrimp

SERVES 4 AS AN APPETIZER

The west bank of New Orleans is home to a sizable Vietnamese population, resulting in some great markets and restaurants. My favorite condiment at these markets is a red garlic chili sauce that goes extremely well with such Louisiana classics as boiled shrimp, especially when combined with fresh mint.

Fresh shrimp are so beautiful in their natural state that it's a shame to peel them before cooking. What's more, they stay firmer, and retain more flavor, when they are cooked in their shell. Don't attempt to eat these shrimp with a knife and fork. (You'd be amazed how many people I've seen attempt this.) Instead, dig in with your hands and drag the peeled shrimp through the spicy, herbaceous marinade.

¼ cup plus 1 teaspoon salt
4 tablespoons Donnie's Spice Mix
  (page 15)
6 bay leaves
1 lemon, cut in half
1 pound medium (16-20 count) shrimp
1 pound ice cubes (about 6 cups)

1 tablespoon Vietnamese garlic chili
  sauce (see Note)
1 cup fresh mint leaves, torn into large
  pieces
1 tablespoon olive oil
Juice of 1 lime

Bring a large pot of water, ¼ cup salt, the spice mix, bay leaves, and lemon halves to a boil and boil for 5 minutes.

Add the shrimp, return to a boil, and cook for 2 minutes. Remove the pot from the heat, add the ice to cool off the shrimp, and allow mixture to soak for 20 minutes. (This way the shrimp absorb the salt and spices without overcooking.) Drain the shrimp in a colander.

In a large bowl, whisk together the garlic chili sauce, mint, 1 teaspoon salt, olive oil, and lime juice. Add the shrimp and toss to combine. Serve immediately or, for a deeper flavor, allow the shrimp to marinate for up to 1 hour before serving.

NOTE: Most people are familiar with sriracha, the Vietnamese red chili sauce that comes in a bottle with a rooster on it. Like sambal, sriracha is strictly chiles and doesn't have much depth to it, just a lot of heat. Vietnamese hot garlic chili sauce is different; it's made from chiles and garlic and has a little bit of sweetness that balances the heat. Both are good pantry staples.

# Louisiana Crawfish Boudin

MAKES ABOUT 1½ POUNDS, OR FOUR 5-INCH LINKS

Although it's difficult for me to fathom, not everyone is a huge fan of pork and liver. So it's no surprise that a more contemporary version of the classic boudin (page 30) was developed using the region's two most important crops: rice and crawfish. In this recipe, which takes considerably less time to make than pork boudin, I reduce the stock to intensify the flavor of the crawfish and allow the sweet meat to break down and marry with the other savory flavors. The result is so delicious and satisfying that every time I make it I wonder why I don't prepare it more often. Crawfish boudin is especially good for outdoor entertaining and picnics on warm Louisiana spring days, since it's not as heavy as the pork variety.

Boudin can also be grilled over really low heat. If you don't want to stuff the sausage into casings, simply shape it into balls, roll in bread crumbs, and deep-fry until golden brown.

If you taste the crawfish mixture right after it's assembled, it will probably seem very spicy. Once it cools, however, the spices settle down. In fact, if you're like me and like food pretty spicy, add an extra pinch of spices. This recipe requires an electric standing mixer fitted with a sausage stuffer attachment.

2 tablespoons butter
1 small onion, finely chopped
1 small poblano chile, stemmed, seeded, and finely chopped (see Note)
1 medium jalapeño pepper, stemmed, seeded, and finely chopped
2 teaspoons minced garlic
1½ tablespoons kosher salt
1 tablespoon dried thyme
1 teaspoon ground black pepper
1 teaspoon chili powder
1 teaspoon paprika

½ teaspoon ground white pepper
4 bay leaves
1 pound Louisiana crawfish tail meat*
2½ cups crawfish, shrimp, or chicken stock
1½ cups long-grain rice
1 bunch scallions, sliced (green and white parts)
½ cup chopped parsley
Hot sauce, to taste
About 3 feet of sausage casings, rinsed

Melt the butter in a large skillet over medium heat. Add the onion, poblano, jalapeño, garlic, salt, thyme, black pepper, chili powder, paprika, white pepper, and bay leaves and cook, stirring, until the vegetables start to soften, about 5 minutes. Add the crawfish and ½ cup of stock and cook, stirring, until the stock has cooked down by two-thirds.

Stir in the rice and an additional 2 cups stock. Cover, reduce heat to low, and simmer very slowly until the rice is cooked, about 20 minutes.

Transfer the cooked rice mixture to a mixing bowl. Add the scallions, parsley, and hot sauce, then mix vigorously by hand for 2 minutes to break down the starch of the rice. (You want the mixture to become slightly starchy and pull together but remain moist.) Using a mixer fitted with the stuffer attachment (without the grinding plate), extrude the mixture into casings, twisting them into 4- to 5-inch links (see Sidebar, page 28).

Bring 2 inches of water to a boil in a deep skillet. Reduce the heat so the water is barely simmering (about 180°F), and add the boudin. Poach for 5 to 7 minutes, just long enough to heat the inside of the sausage. (A lot of stores in Cajun country hold their cooked boudin in a rice cooker full of water.) Refrigerated, crawfish boudin will last for 3 to 4 days. It can be frozen for up to 3 weeks.

NOTE: When chopping chiles, slice them from the inside (rib side) of the pepper for a cleaner cut. If you cut through the thicker skin side, the knife is more likely to slip.

*Any shelled crawfish meat that you purchase will already be cooked.

# Chile-Roasted Shrimp

SERVES 4 AS A MAIN COURSE, 6 TO 8 AS AN APPETIZER

In Louisiana, different sizes of shrimp are typically used for specific dishes. Small shrimp usually end up in gumbos, stews, or étouffées; medium shrimp are for spicy boils, po' boys, and frying (but let's face it, all sizes are good fried). The largest, most beautiful shrimp are saved for special preparations, and they are almost always cooked in the shell. I came up with this simple recipe as an alternative to the more classic barbecued shrimp (made with butter and hot sauce), for a similarly spicy result that doesn't mask the fresh flavor and texture of the shrimp.

I've called for red jalapeños because they are widely available, but my first choice is the fresh paprika chiles that we grow in our garden in New Orleans. If you are ever able to get your hands on them, they are incredible, with a perfect balance of sweetness and heat. If you live in the South, try to grow them—you will never see a plant produce more chiles for a longer season.

1 pound large head-on shrimp
½ cup plus 2 tablespoons olive oil
3 red jalapeño peppers, stemmed (not seeded) and thinly sliced
1 tablespoon salt
1 tablespoon dried oregano

1 teaspoon ground black pepper
Juice of 1 lemon
2 garlic cloves, thinly sliced
1 cup Shrimp Stock (recipe follows) or water
1 tablespoon butter

Combine the shrimp with ½ cup olive oil and the jalapeños, salt, oregano, pepper, lemon juice, and garlic in a large bowl and toss well to mix. Cover with plastic wrap and marinate shrimp at room temperature for 20 minutes, or refrigerate for up to 6 hours.

Preheat the oven as high as it will go, and place the rack in the center of the oven. Place a rimmed baking sheet in the oven for at least 10 minutes so that it gets extremely hot. (My favorite pan to use for this is a thin blue steel pan; they are very cheep and conduct heat really well.) Very carefully remove the hot pan from the oven and gently spread the shrimp across the pan in one even layer—a little crowding is okay. Roast the shrimp until they turn bright pink, 5 to 8 minutes, stirring only once. (Opening the oven too many times will allow too much heat to escape.)

Remove the shrimp from the oven and immediately pour the stock or water over them. Finish with the remaining 2 tablespoons olive oil and butter; toss to coat evenly. The heat of the baking sheet should cause the liquids to bubble and reduce slightly. If the sheet doesn't seem quite hot enough, you can transfer the shrimp to a saucepan and place it over medium-high heat, allowing the sauce to reduce for a minute or two.

Serve the shrimp and sauce with good bread, cold beer, and plenty of napkins.

# Shrimp Stock

MAKES ABOUT 2 QUARTS

Nothing is wasted in the Cajun kitchen, which means that everything from vegetable scraps to seafood shells is put to good use. The heads and shells of fresh shrimp are especially valued, used to make delicious stock for soups, gumbos, and sauces. Shrimp stock gives any shrimp dish *lagniappe*, or that "little something extra." Don't *ever* discard shrimp shells. Store them in a resealable plastic bag and freeze them until you need to cook a batch of broth. (Tightly sealed, they'll last 1 to 3 months in the freezer.)

Searing the shrimp shells before they're simmered and toasting the paprika give this stock a wonderfully deep flavor. The wine adds acidity, which helps balance the flavors. This recipe can be multiplied up or down depending on how many shrimp shells you have to work with.

| | |
|---|---|
| 1 tablespoon vegetable oil | 2 celery stalks, cut into 2-inch lengths |
| Shells and heads (if available) from | 1 small carrot, cut into 1-inch pieces |
|     4 pounds shrimp (about 1¼ pounds | 4 garlic cloves, smashed |
|     shells) | 1 rosemary sprig |
| 1 tablespoon paprika | 8 bay leaves |
| 1 tablespoon ground black pepper | 2 cups dry white wine |
| 1 small onion, quartered | 3 quarts water |

Heat the oil in a large stockpot over high heat. When the oil begins to smoke slightly, add the shells, paprika, and black pepper. Stir frequently for 2 minutes, until the shells crisp up and turn pink.

Add the onion, celery, carrot, garlic, rosemary, and bay leaves. Cook, stirring, for 5 minutes.

Add the white wine and bring to a boil. Reduce liquid by half (about 5 additional minutes), then add water. Return the mixture to a boil, reduce the heat to low, and simmer, skimming off any foam or oil that rises to the surface, for 45 minutes to 1 hour.

Strain the stock, discarding all solids, and ladle into 1-quart containers. The stock can be refrigerated for 3 to 4 days or frozen for up to 2 months.

# Cathy's Shrimp, Corn, and Tomato Stew

SERVES 8 TO 10

When I was growing up, the two most popular soups were gumbo and this shrimp and corn stew. Since we always had so much shrimp in our household, this was a common meal for us, and it is probably one of the first dishes I ever made. There are many different recipes out there for this stew, and while not every one uses a roux, I find the roux gives the stew more character and depth.

The season will determine whether you make this recipe with fresh tomatoes and corn or canned or frozen varieties. My mother-in-law, Cathy Compton, makes hers with canned tomatoes and canned corn with excellent results; outside of summer, you'll get better results with frozen corn and canned tomatoes. But during the peak of summer, when the corn is sweet and the tomatoes are red and juicy, fresh is the way to go.

This recipe will feed at least eight people. My philosophy has always been that, if you're going to go to the trouble to cook something, make plenty for company or leftovers. Like most soups and stews, this dish is even better the next day. I love this hearty stew served over hot steamed rice, but that's the Acadian in me.

4 pounds medium (16–20 count) shrimp, preferably with heads and shells
1 cup (2 sticks) butter
¾ cup all-purpose flour
2 medium onions, finely chopped
4 celery stalks, finely chopped
1 large green bell pepper, cored, seeded, and finely chopped
4 garlic cloves, minced
1 (28-ounce) can diced tomatoes
1 (14-ounce) can diced tomatoes

2½ cups fresh or frozen corn kernels
5 cups Shrimp Stock (page 65)
2 tablespoons salt
2 bay leaves
1½ teaspoons dried basil
½ teaspoon dried thyme
½ teaspoon ground black pepper
¼ teaspoon paprika
½ bunch Italian parsley, finely chopped
1 bunch scallions (white and green parts), finely chopped

Peel the shrimp.

Melt the butter in a large, heavy-bottomed pot over medium heat. Whisk in the flour and cook, whisking almost constantly, just until the roux is a light peanut butter color and the aroma of the roux starts to fill the room, 5 to 10 minutes.

## OIL OR BUTTER ROUX?

My rule of thumb for when to use butter (and not oil) for a roux depends on how dark I want the final result to be. Gumbo, for example, requires a very dark roux, and oil is preferred; butter makes a dark roux bitter. For a light, peanut butter–colored roux like this one, butter is better because it adds a rich nutty taste to the soup. (Some étouffées are made with a butter roux for the same reason.) Dark rouxs are more about using oil as a medium to brown the flour; light rouxs are more about adding a rich, nutty flavor to the dish.

Add the onions, celery, bell pepper, and garlic and cook, stirring, for an additional 5 minutes. Stir in the tomatoes, corn, stock, salt, bay leaves, basil, thyme, pepper, and paprika and bring to a boil. Reduce the heat to low and simmer for 45 minutes, stirring occasionally.

Stir in the peeled shrimp, parsley, and scallions. Bring the stew back to a boil over high heat, then turn the heat to low and simmer for 20 minutes. Remove from the heat, allow stew to stand for 15 minutes to meld flavors, taste and adjust seasonings as desired, and serve.

# Spicy Shrimp Creole

SERVES 6 TO 8 AS A MAIN COURSE

I've been told that spicy food is popular in hot climates because it makes you sweat, which cools you off. I've eaten plenty of spicy food throughout the sweltering Louisiana summers, and I think it just made me hotter—but that's what cold beer is for. All the same, I love to prepare this chile-driven dish in the summer because it makes great use of all the flavorful chiles (poblanos, yellow banana, jalapeño) and ripe, juicy tomatoes that flourish in those months. You may find it hard to believe that the shrimp can shine through these big flavors, but they impart an underlying clean, sweet seafood taste, just as they do in gumbos and stews.

2 pounds medium (16–20 count) head-on
    shrimp
2 tablespoons vegetable oil
1 medium onion, finely chopped
1 celery stalk, finely chopped
2 poblano chiles, stemmed, seeded, and
    finely chopped
1 yellow banana chile, stemmed, seeded,
    and finely chopped
1 jalapeño pepper, stemmed, seeded, and
    finely chopped
2 garlic cloves, thinly sliced
1 teaspoon dried thyme
½ teaspoon dried basil

1½ teaspoons salt
¼ teaspoon ground white pepper
¼ teaspoon ground black pepper
1 (6-ounce) can tomato paste
4 ripe medium tomatoes, finely chopped
    and juice reserved (about 2 cups)
1 tablespoon red wine vinegar
2 cups Shrimp Stock (page 65)
2 tablespoons chopped fresh oregano,
    or 2 teaspoons dried oregano
Perfect Steamed Rice (page 36)
2 scallions (white and green parts), thinly
    sliced
Hot sauce, for garnish (optional)

Peel the shrimp.

Heat the oil in a large cast-iron skillet over medium heat. Add the onion, celery, chiles, garlic, thyme, basil, salt, and white and black pepper, and cook, stirring, until the chiles begin to soften, about 5 minutes. Add the tomato paste and cook, stirring, for 3 minutes more, until the vegetables are well coated.

Add the tomatoes, their juices, and the vinegar. Reduce the heat to low and simmer for 10 minutes, until the mixture is slightly thickened. Add the stock and simmer until the tomatoes break down and begin to form a sauce, 20 minutes more.

Add the peeled shrimp and oregano, and simmer for another 20 minutes, stirring occasionally. Taste for seasonings, then serve immediately over hot rice, garnished with scallions and hot sauce.

# Herbsaint-Infused Oyster Stew with Smoked Bacon

SERVES 6 TO 8 AS A MAIN COURSE, 8 TO 12 AS AN APPETIZER

The first Friday that our restaurant Herbsaint was open after Hurricane Katrina was quite a challenge. Of the forty people whom we normally employ on a weekend night, only seven could make it to the restaurant. My friend John Harris, the chef at Lillette restaurant, called and offered to help in any way he could. He and two of his waiters came to work with us that night, and John acted as a waiter, dishwasher, and bartender. We never expected to be so slammed just five weeks after the worst natural disaster in American history, but we were, and we were running out of food fast. I asked John if he could create a new dish from our comparatively lean pantry. He made this delicious stew in 30 minutes and we sold twenty-five orders in the second half of the night.

This recipe is unique because half the oysters are pureed and used to deepen the oyster flavor in the creamy broth; the other half are added at the end and lightly poached, as a garnish. (If you used all the oysters to flavor the cream, you'd end up with too many overcooked oysters.) You can puree the oysters in a food processor or with a handheld immersion blender; I usually do this in one of my big plastic Mardi Gras beer cups. Also, I use smoked bacon in this dish because I think bacon makes everything taste better; however, it can be left out with great results. If you want a more refined, smooth soup, strain the vegetables from the broth before you add the final oysters. A drizzle of Herbsaint, or another anise-flavored liqueur, pulls the other flavors into focus. Crusty white bread or old-fashioned oyster crackers are the perfect partner for this delicious stew, which will always remind me that good friends soften hard times.

1 pint shucked oysters (about 24 oysters), drained and liquor reserved

3 ounces thick-sliced smoked bacon, cut into ¼-inch cubes

4 tablespoons (½ stick) butter

1 small onion, chopped (¼-inch dice)

1 bunch scallions

2 celery stalks, chopped (¼-inch dice)

1 cup chopped (¼-inch dice) fennel bulb (about 1 small bulb)

2 garlic cloves, finely minced

5 bay leaves, preferably fresh

½ teaspoon salt

¼ teaspoon cayenne pepper

1 teaspoon ground black pepper

1 teaspoon chopped fresh thyme

⅓ cup all-purpose flour

1 small russet potato, peeled and diced

2 cups heavy cream

2 tablespoons Herbsaint or other anise-flavored liqueur

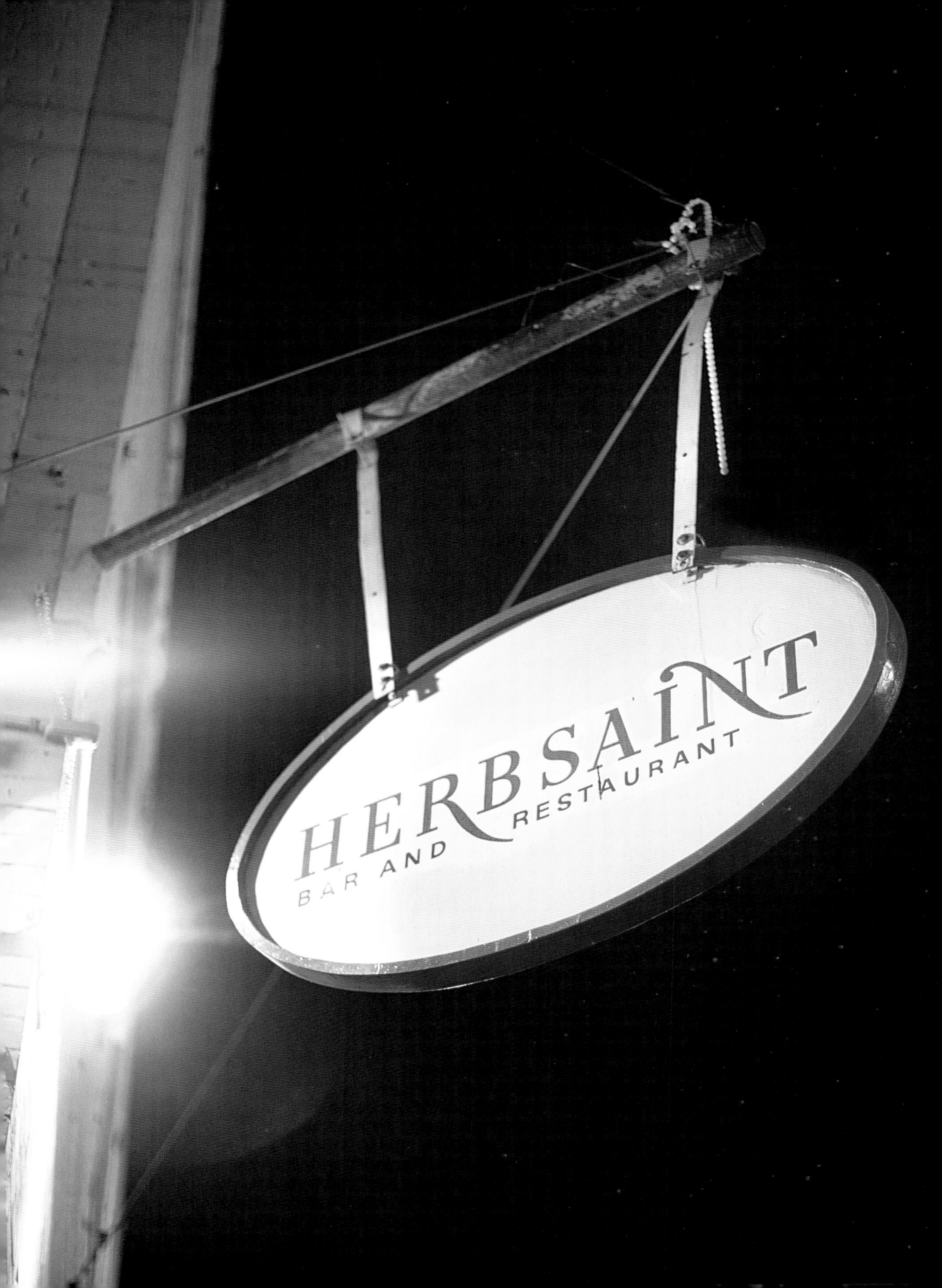
HERBSAINT
BAR AND RESTAURANT

Pick through the oysters to ensure they are clean of grit or shell. Place half the oysters in a food processor and puree until smooth (or place in a plastic cup or bowl and use an immersion blender, as described above). Transfer the puree to a bowl and refrigerate along with remaining whole oysters until needed.

Heat the bacon in a large pot or Dutch oven over low heat until its fat is rendered and the bacon is just starting to sizzle, 2 to 3 minutes. Add 1 tablespoon of butter and the onion, scallions, celery, fennel, garlic, bay leaves, salt, cayenne, black pepper, and thyme. Cook slowly, stirring frequently, until they are tender—about 10 minutes. You want to "sweat" the vegetables, so they soften and release their juices, without browning them.

Add 2 more tablespoons of butter to the pot. As soon as the butter melts, add the flour and stir until ingredients are evenly coated. Add 2 cups reserved oyster liquor (see Note), the potato, and pureed oysters and bring to a simmer. Simmer gently for 15 minutes. Add 1 cup of cream and simmer for 5 more minutes.

To finish the stew, add the last cup of cream, remaining tablespoon of butter, Herbsaint, and reserved whole oysters. Cook for 5 more minutes and serve.

NOTE: If you do not have enough oyster liquor from the pint of oysters, add fish stock, chicken broth, or water, as needed. Alternatively, some seafood markets sell oyster liquor, which is another great option.

# Crab Cakes with Jalapeño Remoulade

SERVES 4

I have a list of things that I almost never order in a restaurant, and crab cakes head the list. Too often they are made with low-quality crab meat and taste more like wet bread than crab. For those craving the real deal, look no further: This recipe creates entirely different crab cakes. They are both rich and zippy, thanks to the chile, scallions, mustard, and dashes of hot sauce and lemon juice. The Jalapeño Remoulade truly sends them over the edge.

The most important thing to remember when making crab cakes is to not overwork the mixture. The cakes should be loose, just *barely* holding together. Chilling them before they are cooked helps firm up them and hold together without too much binder (bread crumbs).

Dungeness and Peeky Toe crab can be used in this recipe, but my favorite is blue crab from the Gulf. I have actually gone to the trouble of cooking live crabs and picking them myself, but trust me—if you can buy good lump crab, that's the easier way to go. Even for a pretty accomplished crab picker like me, it takes a while to get enough for these cakes—maybe because I always eat half of it before it ever gets into the bowl.

1 pound best-quality lump crab meat (not pasteurized)
1 tablespoon butter
½ small onion, finely chopped
½ poblano chile, stemmed, seeded, and finely chopped
1 garlic clove, minced
1 teaspoon salt
¼ teaspoon pure chile powder (like ancho, New Mexico, or chipotle)
¼ teaspoon ground black pepper
¼ teaspoon cayenne
1 egg, lightly beaten

¼ cup mayonnaise
1 teaspoon Creole (or whole-grain) mustard
Several dashes of Louisiana hot sauce
1 scallion (white and green parts), finely chopped
2 tablespoons chopped Italian parsley
Juice of ½ lemon
¾ cup fresh bread crumbs
2 tablespoons vegetable oil, plus more as needed
Jalapeño Remoulade (recipe follows)

Place the crab meat in a large mixing bowl and carefully pick through for shells (see Note, page 82), then set aside.

Melt the butter in a medium skillet over medium heat. Add the onion, poblano, garlic, salt, chile powder, black pepper, and cayenne and cook, stirring, until the vegetables are softened but not brown, 3 to 4 minutes. Transfer the vegetable mixture to a mixing bowl and set aside to cool for about 15 minutes.

Add the crab, the egg, mayonnaise, mustard, hot sauce, scallion, parsley, lemon juice, and ¼ cup of the bread crumbs to the vegetable mixture. Using your hands, gently combine the ingredients.

Using a 1-cup measuring cup, form the mixture into cakes, packing gently; they should look like hockey pucks, about 2 inches thick with straight sides. Cover the cakes and chill for 20 to 30 minutes, or overnight.

When you are ready to cook the crab cakes, place the remaining ½ cup bread crumbs in a pie tin. Dredge both sides of each cake in the crumbs, shaking off the excess. Heat 2 tablespoons of vegetable oil in a large skillet over medium-high heat. When the oil is hot but not smoking, fry the crab cakes for 4 to 5 minutes on each side, until golden brown. Do not overcrowd the pan—fry in batches if necessary, adding more oil if needed. Serve immediately, with Jalapeño Remoulade.

## Jalapeño Remoulade

MAKES ABOUT 1¼ CUPS

For the best results, make this spicy condiment a few hours in advance and then cover and refrigerate, so the flavors have time to develop.

1 small jalapeño pepper, stemmed, seeded, and finely chopped
1 bunch scallions (white parts only), thinly sliced
1 cup mayonnaise
½ teaspoon salt
¼ teaspoon ground black pepper
¼ teaspoon crushed red pepper flakes
2 teaspoons red wine vinegar
Juice of 1 lime

Whisk together all the ingredients in a mixing bowl; cover and refrigerate until needed.

# Cameron Parish Stuffed Crabs

SERVES 6

Childhood amusements could be a bit dangerous in southwestern Louisiana, but they yielded delicious results. When we were kids, my sister and I often went to the Sabine National Wildlife Refuge in Cameron to go "crabbing." This involved standing on the side of the road in stifling 98°F weather, next to a canal full of alligators, and attempting to lure crabs to the shore using raw chicken pieces tied to a string. Needless to say, we kept a really good eye on the 'gators to make sure they didn't follow that chicken onto the bank.

Cleaning crabs is a labor of love; it's not my favorite thing to do unless I'm eating them at a boil. In this recipe, we use the blue crabs for both their sweet meat and beautiful shells (the top of the shell makes a stunning serving dish); the remaining shells and scraps create a stock rich with crab goodness. But because I like my stuffed crab brimming with meat, and I don't have the patience to clean an additional twenty or so crabs, I supplement the filling with a half-pound of packaged lump crab meat.

Be sure to save all your vegetable scraps, including the onion skins, celery and pepper trimmings (even the seeds and stems), and parsley stems, as you can use them to make the crab stock.

Salt
6 blue crabs
½ small onion, finely chopped
1 celery stalk, finely chopped
½ green bell pepper, cored, seeded, and finely chopped
1 jalapeño pepper, stemmed, seeded, and minced
3 scallions (white and green parts), thinly sliced
2 tablespoons thinly sliced Italian parsley

4 to 6 bay leaves
5 tablespoons butter
¼ teaspoon cayenne pepper
¼ teaspoon ground white pepper
Pinch of ground black pepper
1 cup dry bread crumbs
1 (½ pound) container lump crab meat, picked through for shells (not pasteurized; also, see Note, page 82)
2 dashes of hot sauce
Juice of ½ lemon
1 egg, lightly beaten

Bring a large pot of generously salted water to a boil. Add the crabs and boil for 10 minutes, then drain in a colander and cool. When the crabs are cool enough to handle, hold each one over a bowl as you pull off the top shell; this way you catch all the flavorful juices that run out. Set the top shells aside and pour the reserved crab juice into a stockpot.

In the middle of the "topless" crab, you will find the crab fat, which will be orange and yellow (this is really good stuff), as well as the lungs, or "dead man's fingers," as they're called in these parts. Pull out the lungs and discard; remove the fat and reserve in a small bowl. Gently break the crabs where the legs meet the body, remove the meat, and reserve, tossing the shells into the stockpot as you go.

Add the vegetable peelings and skins, parsley stems, and bay leaves to the stockpot and add enough water to just cover the shells. Simmer over medium heat for about 45 minutes. Strain the stock and discard the shells and vegetables. You should have about ½ cup stock. If you have more than that, return the strained stock to the pot and simmer until it's reduced to ½ cup.

In a large sauté pan, heat 2 tablespoons butter with the reserved crab fat over medium heat. Add the onion, celery, green pepper, jalapeño, 1 teaspoon salt, the cayenne, white and black pepper. Cook for about 7 minutes, until the vegetables are soft.

Add the reduced crab stock and simmer for 2 minutes over low heat. Transfer this mixture to a mixing bowl and cool for 10 minutes.

Add ½ cup of bread crumbs, the picked lump and blue crab, the hot sauce, lemon juice, and egg. Combine gently so you don't shred the crab meat. Divide this mixture evenly among the reserved crab shells.

Preheat the oven to 350°F.

Combine the remaining ½ cup bread crumbs, 3 tablespoons butter, the scallions, and parsley and sprinkle the mixture over the top of the stuffed crabs—use your fingers to gently press them onto the stuffing. Bake for 10 to 15 minutes, until the bread crumbs brown and the crab is hot in the middle.

# Grilled Redfish "On the Half-Shell"

SERVES 6

Like most of the people from this area, I have done my share of fish filleting. Redfish, one of the most popular local varieties, is a clean-tasting white fish that is similar to bass. I love it because it has great moisture content without being fatty. Redfish are particularly challenging to clean, though, because they have large scales that are tough to remove. Needless to say, I was excited when a local fisherman showed me this clever cooking method in which the fish is grilled with its scales on. The scales harden and create a nifty "shell" that protects the delicate meat from direct contact with the heat *and* retains the natural juices to keep the fish moist. The sturdy scales also help prevent the fish from sticking to the grill, a serious side benefit.

Don't even think of a heavy sauce for this recipe. Simply season the fish with salt, lemon juice, fresh parsley, garlic, and olive oil and enjoy the spectacularly fresh flavor. If you can't find redfish, the "half shell" method also delivers delicious results with drum, branzino, pompano, rockfish, red snapper, and salmon.

6 (7-ounce) fillets of redfish, skin and scales on, with pin bones removed
1½ teaspoons kosher salt
Scant 1½ teaspoons ground black pepper
Scant 1½ teaspoons red pepper flakes

4 garlic cloves, very thinly sliced
½ cup good quality extra-virgin olive oil
1 tablespoon coarse sea salt
½ cup chopped Italian parsley
Two large lemons, halved

Rinse the fish fillets and pat them dry with paper towels. Place the fillets on a baking sheet, season with the salt, pepper, and red pepper flakes. Top the fillets with the sliced garlic and drizzle with half of the olive oil. Use your fingers to distribute the oil and seasonings evenly over fish, then set the fish aside to marinate while you heat the grill.

Fire up your grill to a medium-high setting. (If you are using charcoal, the coals should be mostly white.) Place the fillets scale side down on the hot grill. Cover the grill and cook the fish *without moving* for 7 to 10 minutes, until it is just cooked through; it will flake easily when tested with a paring knife. (You can also cook the fish "on the half shell" on an oiled baking sheet in a 475°F oven for 6 to 8 minutes.)

Using a metal spatula, transfer the fillets to serving plates and top with the sea salt and parsley, a little extra olive oil, and lemon juice.

## Fishing with Grandad Adams

My grandad had an old bass boat that wasn't kept up very well. His tackle box and the lures in it were always a jumbled, rusty mess. I always hoped he wouldn't ask me to get anything out of it, because I knew it was going to be a long, arduous process of untangling rusty treble hooks. My father tells me that Grandaddy used to bait the waters and mark the spot in such a way that only he could find it again. The man could catch fish—and lots of them.

During the day we fished for bream and catfish. The way he prepared them is still my absolute favorite way to eat fish. The fish were headed, scaled, gutted, dredged in cornmeal, and shallow-fried in bacon fat. My wife and I recently cooked bream this way when we went camping in Alabama. We were at a primitive site by a lake. Like a good Louisiana boy, I had packed my cast-iron skillet and cornmeal. We caught some bream, placed the skillet directly on the campfire coals, and fried them up. Awesome.

I was around fourteen when I got to spend my first and only night alone with Grandad Adams at Toledo Bend. He took me out on the lake at night to a spot under a bridge to catch white perch. My job was to stand at the bow of the boat with the flashlight and look for stumps. I remember hoping that he didn't throw the boat in reverse to try to make me fall in (a favorite "joke"). When we got to the bridge, he dropped two car headlights fitted inside a foam floating device facedown into the water. The lights attract the fish to the bait. We waited 20 minutes before we hooked up our lines. (I still tie my hook the way he taught me.) He put three lines in the water, I put in one, and a feeding frenzy began. I rushed madly to take my fish off the hook, rebait, and get the line back in. He was next to me doing it with three lines at a time, all of them with fish on the hook, while he was smoking and talking to himself. To this day, I have never caught so many fish in such a short time. We filled two ice chests in 40 minutes.

The most memorable part of that night, though, was not the fishing but the conversation. I can't think about that night without getting choked up, mainly because all these years later, I wonder why I didn't spend more time getting to know this man. We talked for hours. Or, I should say, I asked questions and *he* talked for hours.

I have often dreamed of being able to live that life—cooking for my family with ingredients that I've gathered myself. In a way, as the chef of my two restaurants, I have gotten close to it. I have other people growing vegetables and fishing for me, but I do get to cook these fantastic ingredients for other people, and I get paid for it. I guess I can't imagine doing anything other than cooking. My entire life has revolved around it. I wonder what my son and daughter will think of my cooking when they are older. Teaching young, aspiring cooks in the restaurant is rewarding, but the opportunity to teach my kids to cook, and to pass on Grandad's food, is a feeling I cannot even put into words.

# Summer Crab and Tomato Salad

SERVES 4 AS A LUNCH OR APPETIZER

As much as I love warm, bubbling crab dishes, I still favor my crabmeat cold and "dressed" in mayo, especially when it's super-fresh and in luxuriously large pieces. The acidity of ripe tomatoes is a natural combination with the crab's clean seafood flavor and a rich, creamy dressing. Peppery watercress, simply dressed with oil and vinegar, makes a great addition on the side and creates a well-rounded salad for a lunch or first course.

1 jalapeño pepper, stemmed, seeded, and finely chopped
Zest and juice of 1 lime
1 tablespoon white wine vinegar
3 tablespoons mayonnaise
12 mint leaves, finely chopped
½ teaspoon salt

½ teaspoon red pepper flakes
Generous pinch of cayenne pepper
1 pound jumbo lump crab meat, carefully picked over for shells and cartilage (not pasteurized; see Note)
2 large ripe tomatoes
Sea salt

Combine the jalapeño, lime zest and juice, and vinegar in the bowl of a food processor and puree until smooth. Transfer to a medium bowl and fold in the mayonnaise, mint, salt, red pepper flakes, and cayenne.

Add the crab to the dressing and gently fold together. Slice the tomatoes a little shy of ½-inch thick. Divide the tomatoes among four salad plates and season with salt. Top the tomatoes with equal portions of the crab salad and serve immediately.

NOTE: When picking over lump crab meat for bits of shell or cartilage, take your time and try to keep the crab in big chunks. It will break down a bit when you combine the meat with the other ingredients, so the less handling early on, the better. One time at Herbsaint we had 10 pounds of some of the most beautiful white crab meat I'd ever seen. Without consulting anyone, one of the prep cooks decided to pick through it, and he tore it to shreds. It looked as if someone had put the crab through a food processor and then ran it over with a car. Of course, then I had to kill him.

# Crispy Soft-Shell Crab
# with Chili Glaze and Mint Coleslaw

SERVES 4

When I lived in San Francisco, I frequently ate at an old-school Hong Kong–style seafood restaurant that served Dungeness crabs coated in a spicy, sticky paste of garlic and chili sauce.

Back in New Orleans, I craved the same flavors, so I decided to try it with soft-shell crabs, and give the dish a Vietnamese spin by serving them with fresh mint coleslaw, a nice cooling counterpart to the spicy glaze. Instead of using straight chili sauce, I combine the chili paste with butter to use as a coating for the soft-shells.

We serve these crispy, spicy crabs at both Herbsaint and Cochon as a seasonal special during late spring and summer. Every night that they're on the menu, we sell out.

Chile butter
½ pound (2 sticks) butter, at room
    temperature
2 tablespoons Vietnamese garlic chili
    sauce (see Note, page 60)
1 tablespoon sriracha (see Note, page 60)
1 tablespoon honey
2 teaspoons chopped garlic
½ teaspoons cayenne pepper
1 teaspoon Asian seedless red pepper
    flakes (see Note) or standard red
    pepper flakes

1 teaspoon fresh lemon juice
½ teaspoon salt

4 soft-shell crabs, cleaned (see Sidebar)
Salt and pepper
Peanut oil, for frying
2 cups all-purpose flour
3 cups buttermilk
Mint Coleslaw (recipe follows)

To make the chile butter, use a rubber spatula to combine all the ingredients in a mixing bowl. Set aside at room temperature so it stays soft (not melted).

Place the crabs on paper towels so that they stay dry. Season with salt and pepper.

Heat 4 inches of oil in a Dutch oven over medium-high heat. When the oil is very hot, dredge the crabs in flour, dip in buttermilk, and then run them back through the flour again. (Use a big, wide bowl for the flour so that you have plenty of room to work with.)

## CLEANING SOFT-SHELL CRABS

Place each crab belly side down. Gently lift up one side of the top shell to reveal the lungs. With a pair of scissors, cut the lungs out. Repeat for the other side. Next, locate the eyeballs; underneath the eyeballs is the front or mouth of the crab. With one snip, cut the eyes and the mouth off.

Add the crabs to the oil two or three at a time so that the oil temperature doesn't drop and make your crabs soggy. Fry each batch for 5 to 7 minutes, flipping the crabs once, until the bubbling subsides and they have a nice golden color. Transfer to a plate lined with paper towels and blot dry. Repeat with the remaining crabs.

Place 2 to 4 tablespoons of the chile butter (as desired), per crab, in the bottom of a large mixing bowl. Add one hot crab and gently swirl the bowl around to coat the crab with the butter. (You can also use a pastry brush to paint the butter on the crab.) Do this step quickly; the crab should be in the butter just long enough to coat and not to completely melt the butter. Repeat for other crabs and serve with the coleslaw alongside.

## Mint Coleslaw

1 cup mayonnaise
½ teaspoon salt, or more as needed
¼ teaspoon ground black pepper
¼ teaspoon red pepper flakes
2 teaspoons red wine vinegar
Juice of 1 lime
1 large jalapeño pepper, stemmed, seeded, and finely chopped
1 bunch scallions (white and green parts), minced
1 small napa cabbage, thinly sliced (about 4 cups)
1 cup mint leaves, torn into large pieces
1 large carrot, peeled and grated

Whisk together the mayonnaise, salt, black pepper, red pepper flakes, vinegar, lime juice, jalapeño, and scallions in a large mixing bowl. (Alternatively, puree the scallions, jalapeño, lime juice, vinegar, and seasonings in a food processor, then transfer to a mixing bowl and fold in the mayonnaise.) Add the cabbage, mint, and carrot and toss until well coated. Taste for seasonings and add more salt as desired.

FAMILY GATHERINGS

Friends, family, and good food are inseparable in Cajun Country. Whether the occasion is a holiday, family reunion, football game, Sunday chicken fry, or even a funeral, eating well—and eating plenty—is the tie that binds year-round.

Autumn is my absolute favorite time of the year. The day the first cool breeze rustles the leaves on the magnolia and sweet olive trees, bringing what we all hope is the end of the long, sweltering summer, is a magical one in Louisiana. With that nip in the air comes a lot of great stuff: the end of hurricane season, the beginning of football season, and especially the holidays (did I mention the end of the long, hot summer?). All this means my two favorite things in the world: food and family. I love the way the house smells when it's buried in the rich aromas of roasted meats and freshly baked pies, and the way it feels to yearn for those tastes the entire day as the meal is being prepared.

My grandparents, my mom, and my mother-in-law all prepared fantastic holiday dinners. Cooking these special meals is now my responsibility, and it's is the biggest honor I will ever have as a chef—it's more satisfying than any award or busy night at the restaurant. I mostly gravitate to the classics, because the holidays just aren't the same without creamy mashed potatoes, insanely rich green bean casserole, and roasted duck with a sticky orange glaze. I can't imagine Thanksgiving without oyster cornbread stuffing and giblet gravy with bacon. And what would that weekend be without a hot turkey sandwich, smothered in leftover gravy, the next day?

I had to include my Super Bowl dishes in this chapter because, I'll be honest, Super Bowl Sunday is my favorite day of the year, the holiday we spend with the friends whom we consider family. Back in the day, the football games—and our parties—were decidedly rough. Now that we all have kids of our own, the focus has shifted to food: my seafood gumbo (served with a scoop of mustardy potato salad) and choucroute with sausage and duck confit. It's not such a bad trade-off.

Even funerals offer the opportunity to eat well. In Cajun Country, nobody brings finger foods to funerals. They bring full-on, holiday-style meals. Traditionally, people offer their signature dishes to the grieving family; some folks are famous for their jambalaya, some for shrimp casserole, and my uncle Robert is known for his smoked brisket. Granny usually made either rice dressing or gumbo, and I remember her gumbo in particular. In small towns like Sulphur, people get to know what others specialize in, so buffet menus are balanced out surprisingly well. There's so much food at Cajun funerals that families generally don't have to cook for three days.

These recipes are meant to feed a crowd, so you can throw a party or enjoy amazing leftovers.

# Fried Chicken Livers
# with Hot Pepper Glaze

SERVES 4

The first chicken livers I ever ate were out of a KFC bucket (back in the old days it was pretty common for them to be included). It was love at first bite, and I've been eating them ever since. Chicken livers are one of those foods that people either love or hate, and this recipe has converted a lot of haters. The secret is in balancing the strong, rich taste of liver with something sweet and/or vinegary. This dish uses vinegar, along with some sharp fresh herbs to accent the combination. When we put this dish on the opening menu at Cochon, I never thought anyone would order it, but it's turned out to be one of our most popular dishes.

1 pound chicken livers (about 12 to 15)
1 cup buttermilk
1 tablespoon hot sauce
Salt
Ground black pepper
Peanut oil or lard, for frying
4 slices white bread, crust trimmed
1 tablespoon melted butter

2 cups all-purpose flour
2 mint sprigs
Leaves from 3 or 4 flat-leaf parsley sprigs
½ small onion, very thinly sliced
1 tablespoon olive oil
1 tablespoon sherry vinegar
¾ cup Hot Pepper Jelly (recipe follows)

Preheat the oven to 350°F.

In a medium bowl, combine the chicken livers, buttermilk, hot sauce, 1 teaspoon salt, and ½ teaspoon pepper and marinate at least 1 hour or overnight in the fridge.

Heat the oil in a large, deep pot to 350°F.

Meanwhile, cut each bread slice into four equal squares, brush with butter, and season with salt and pepper. Place on a baking sheet and toast until golden brown, 5 to 7 minutes.

Place the flour in a shallow dish. One at a time, lift the livers out of the marinade, shaking to remove excess buttermilk, and coat in the flour, shaking off excess.

Fry the chicken livers in small batches for 2 to 3 minutes, until golden brown and just cooked through; transfer to a plate lined with paper towels. To serve, place 4 toast points on a plate and top each with a fried liver. Toss the mint, parsley, and onion with the oil and vinegar. Spread 1 teaspoon of pepper jelly over each liver and top with some of the salad.

# Hot Pepper Jelly

MAKES 4 CUPS

This jelly also perks up roast duck dishes, and it's also surprisingly good with fried seafood. At Susan Spicer's restaurant Bayona, she uses pepper jelly to make a great sauce for seared duck breast.

2 red bell peppers
10 jalapeño peppers
1½ cups white distilled vinegar
1½ cups apple juice
1 (1¾ ounces) box powdered pectin
½ teaspoon salt
5 cups sugar

Remove the stems and seeds from the peppers and cut into half-inch pieces. Combine the peppers with the vinegar in a blender and puree. Transfer to a 1-quart container, add the apple juice, and refrigerate overnight to develop flavor. Make sure there are 4 cups; if not, add enough apple juice to make 4 cups. Add the pectin and salt, and bring to a boil over medium heat while stirring. Add sugar and return to a rolling boil for 1 minute while stirring. Remove from heat and skim any foam that has risen to the surface. Ladle into four hot sterilized 8-ounce canning jars (see Note), seal, and process according to the jar manufacturer's instructions. Let cool on a rack and check that jars have sealed properly.

NOTE: It's essential to wash canning jars, lids, and screw bands in hot, soapy water, then rinse well. Use a clean towel to dry the bands. To sterilize, place the empty jars on a rack in a boiling-water canner or a deep 8- to 10-quart pot and add enough hot water to cover by 2 inches. Bring to a boil, then boil for 10 minutes. Remove the canner from heat, leaving the jars in the water, covered. Similarly, heat the lids in water to cover by 2 inches in a small saucepan until a thermometer registers 180°F (do not let boil). Remove from heat. Keep jars and lids submerged in hot water, covered, until ready to use.

# Chicken and Rice Soup

SERVES 6 TO 8

As far as I'm concerned, this is one of the world's best comfort dishes, especially if you're under the weather. This is a very easy recipe to prepare, especially if you already have some chicken broth in your freezer. Simmering the chicken broth slowly with a roasted chicken develops a rich, concentrated chicken flavor that makes this soup extraordinary. As with gumbo and other soups, this one is even better on the second day.

In a pinch you can make this soup with a store-bought roasted chicken and some low-sodium chicken broth, which will cut the prep time down by more than half and still yield delicious results.

1 roasted chicken

3 quarts chicken broth

2 tablespoons butter or reserved chicken fat (see instructions)

1 small onion, diced

3 celery stalks, diced

4 small carrots, diced

12 cremini mushrooms, thickly sliced

4 garlic cloves, thinly sliced

8 bay leaves

1 bunch scallions (green and white parts), chopped

1 tablespoon salt

1 teaspoon ground black pepper

2 teaspoon dried oregano

2 to 3 cups cooked rice

If you have roasted the chicken yourself, set the drippings aside to allow the fat to rise to the surface. Pick the chicken meat from the bones (discard skin) and chop into ½-inch chunks, cover, and refrigerate. Transfer the chicken carcass to a stockpot and add 3 quarts broth. Bring the broth to a boil, skim as necessary, reduce the heat to low, and then simmer for 1½ hours. Strain the broth and reserve.

Heat 2 tablespoons of butter (or the same amount of chicken fat, skimmed from the top of the pan drippings) in a large pot or Dutch oven over medium heat. Add the onion, celery, carrots, mushrooms, garlic, bay leaves, scallions, salt, pepper, and oregano and cook, stirring for a few minutes, until the vegetables soften; they should not brown. Add the strained chicken broth and the diced chicken. Bring the soup to a boil, then reduce the heat and simmer 30 to 40 minutes, until the chicken starts to break down and meld with the stock. When the soup is finished, add the rice, taste for seasonings, and adjust salt and pepper as desired and serve.

NOTE: You can also scoop the rice individually into serving bowls and ladle the soup on top if you don't want to add it to the soup all at once (the rice will thicken the soup overnight and make the liquid a bit more cloudy).

# Aunt Cynthia's Tomato and Bacon Pie (aka Cajun Pizza)

SERVES 6 TO 8

When we were kids we used to visit my aunt Cynthia on the Alabama coast (before it was filled with condos and hotels). Aunt Cynthia and her sister Aunt Sally are both amazing cooks, as Grandad was.

Whenever I see Aunt Cynthia these days, we talk about food: how she prepares her collard greens and her fried chicken, and this irresistible savory pie, which happens to be a favorite of Aunt Sally's. At first blush this recipe sounds a little strange, but the combination is amazing, not unlike the layering of tomatoes, onions, bacon, and cheese on a hamburger.

When cutting pies like this that have a rather loose filling, use a long, sharp knife and slice in long, even strokes.

Tomato and Bacon Pie is great for a potluck dinner, or for a side dish for roast meat dinners. The success of this pie will be directly related to the quality of the tomatoes that you use, so be sure to find the ripest ones you can find. (Heirloom varieties from the farmers' market would be an excellent choice.)

12 ounces sliced bacon
2 ripe medium tomatoes, cut into ¼-inch slices
1 (9-inch) prebaked Pie Crust (recipe follows), cooked

Salt and pepper
½ small onion, thinly sliced
5 ounces Cheddar or pepper jack cheese, grated

Cook the bacon in a skillet until crisp and set aside to cool on paper towels or a brown paper bag. (Twelve ounces is probably a little more than you will need, but somehow a few extra pieces always get eaten.)

Preheat the oven to 375°F.

Place a layer of tomato slices on the bottom of the crust and season lightly with salt and pepper. Top with a layer of onion slices and cheese. Repeat this process two more times.

Crumble the cooked bacon over the top layer of onion and cheese and bake for about 25 minutes, until the cheese has melted and the tomatoes have released some of their moisture. Place the pie on a wire rack and allow it to cool completely.

# Pie Crust

2 tablespoons butter
2 tablespoons lard or vegetable shortening
¼ teaspoon salt
1¼ cups all-purpose flour
3 tablespoons ice water

Using a fork or your fingers, cut the butter, lard, and salt into the flour until the mixture resembles coarse pebbles. Make a well in the middle of the mixture and add water. Knead for about 30 seconds until dough comes together. Roll the dough out on a floured surface until it's ¼-inch thick and shape into a rustic free-form circle or gently drape it into a buttered pie pan and trim as necessary. Refrigerate the crust until needed.

Preheat the oven to 350°F.

Using a fork, prick the bottom of the pie in several places and bake for 25 minutes, or until lightly browned.

NOTE: Pie crusts generally will bake more evenly when they are cold, so place the crust in the freezer for about 20 minutes before baking.

# Eggplant Rice Dressing

SERVES 6 TO 8 AS A SIDE DISH, 2 TO 4 AS A MAIN COURSE

My grandmother passed along this recipe verbally, in the same fashion as most other recipes were handed down in the family. This leads to a lot of assumptions being made, particularly with respect to seasonings. Contrary to popular belief, the "spice" in many Cajun recipes is merely salt and pepper, with the occasional kick of cayenne.

Eggplant Rice Dressing makes an excellent (and easy) one-pot meal or side dish (it's great alongside roasted or fried chicken). It's also a great contribution to a potluck. In Cajun Country, it's a staple at holidays, funerals, and family reunions.

I don't think many people can resist the way luscious sautéed eggplant melds with rice, ground beef, and aromatics to create this rich, satisfying dressing. Using water instead of chicken broth allows the true flavor of the eggplant to shine.

I've kept this recipe pretty simple to showcase the eggplant, but feel free to add some chopped green or red peppers or celery (along with the onion) to punch it up a little.

1 large eggplant, diced (not peeled)
1 tablespoon vegetable oil or lard
1 pound ground beef
1 medium onion, finely chopped
5 garlic cloves, minced
1½ tablespoons salt
2 teaspoons ground black pepper

1½ teaspoons cayenne pepper
2 cups long-grain rice
1 bunch scallions (white and green
    parts), coarsely chopped
4 bay leaves
3 cups water

Bring a large pot of water to a boil. Add the eggplant, return to a boil for 1 minute, then drain in a colander.

Heat the oil or lard in a large Dutch oven over medium-high heat. Add the meat and cook, stirring, until the meat browns, about 5 minutes. Add the onion, garlic, salt, pepper, and cayenne and sauté for an additional 3 minutes.

Stir in the eggplant, the rice, scallions, and bay leaves. Add the water and stir together gently. Bring the mixture to a boil, then reduce the heat to low, cover, and cook for 25 to 30 minutes. Be sure to use a cover that seals the pot tightly or the rice will not cook evenly. When the rice is tender, remove from the heat and allow the dish to sit, covered, for another 5 to 10 minutes (this way any excess moisture will be absorbed). Serve immediately, or let the dressing cool, uncovered, for about 10 minutes and then cover to keep warm.

# Shrimp and Eggplant Dressing

SERVES 8 TO 10

Cajun food is unique in the way that it melds ingredients and turns them into something that is more than the sum of its parts. This dish is one such example. It combines staple southern Louisiana ingredients like shrimp, cornbread, and eggplant and creates a flavor that is entirely new. The shrimp is used in an economical way, as a flavor enhancer that balances the sweetness of the cornbread and the earthiness of the eggplant. This dressing is the perfect potluck dish because it's so satisfying, and you can be pretty sure that no one else is bringing it, making it a good conversation piece.

3½ pounds unpeeled medium shrimp (21-26 count), head and tail on
2 large eggplants
½ cup plus 2 tablespoons vegetable oil
2 tablespoons butter, plus more for the baking dish
1 large onion, chopped
1 green bell pepper, cored, seeded, and finely chopped
1 poblano chile, stemmed, seeded, and finely chopped
3 celery stalks, finely chopped
4 garlic cloves, minced
1 tablespoon plus 1 teaspoon salt
1 tablespoon dried oregano

1½ teaspoons chili powder
1 teaspoon paprika
1½ teaspoons ground black pepper
½ teaspoon cayenne pepper
¼ teaspoon ground white pepper
2½ cups Shrimp Stock (page 65)
½ recipe Crusty Cornbread (page 173), preferably day-old
1 bunch scallions (green and white parts), thinly sliced
½ bunch parsley, coarsely chopped (about ¾ cup)
3 large eggs, lightly beaten
Several dashes of hot sauce, to taste
Juice of ½ lemon

Peel the shrimp and reserve the heads and shells for making stock.

Preheat the oven and a large roasting pan to 500°F for at least 15 minutes. Meanwhile, peel the eggplant in ½-inch vertical stripes, leaving equal portions of the skin in between. (If you peel the entire eggplant, there is not enough texture, but leaving the eggplant unpeeled makes for too much tough skin.) Cut the eggplant into ½-inch cubes.

When the pan is hot, add the vegetable oil and return to the oven until the oil is very hot, about 5 minutes. Carefully add the eggplant to the pan, stir to coat evenly with oil, and spread in an even layer. Roast until cooked through, stirring and turning occasionally.

Grease a 9 x 13-inch baking dish with butter.

In a large skillet, heat the butter over medium-high heat. Add the onion, peppers, celery, and garlic and sauté until softened. Add the salt, oregano, chili powder, paprika, black pepper, cayenne, and white pepper and sauté for 2 minutes. Add the shrimp and cook until just cooked through, about 5 minutes.

Add the roasted eggplant and ½ cup of stock. Simmer until the eggplant-shrimp mixture is almost dry. Add remaining 2 cups stock and bring to a simmer. Add the cornbread, scallions, and parsley and stir to combine. Remove from the heat and let cool slightly, then stir in the lightly beaten eggs, hot sauce, and lemon juice. Transfer the mixture to the prepared baking dish. Bake until firm and a golden crust forms on top, 45 minutes to 1 hour.

# Lake Charles Dirty Rice

SERVES 6 TO 8

This recipe appears at just about every occasion in Cajun Country. Whether it's a holiday, funeral, family reunion, or potluck dinner, you can bet there will be at least one form of dirty rice or rice dressing. At the Link family reunion in Robert's Cove, I counted six different versions, all different. The essential ingredients are few, but flavor and texture vary greatly.

The main difference between dirty rice and rice dressing is that rice dressing is generally made with ground beef or pork, whereas dirty rice is made with pork and chicken livers. Many people think they don't like liver, but when it's balanced with other flavors, the liver taste is not overpowering. I've served this deeply flavored rice to many people who claim they hate liver, only to have them love it.

2 tablespoons canola oil

4 ounces ground pork

½ cup chicken livers (about 4 ounces), pureed

1½ teaspoons salt

½ teaspoon ground black pepper

½ teaspoon chili powder

1½ cups chicken broth

1 small onion, finely chopped

2 celery stalks, finely chopped

2 garlic cloves, minced

1 jalapeño pepper, stemmed, seeded, and finely chopped

1 tablespoon dried oregano

3 cups Perfect Steamed Rice (page 36) or other cooked rice

½ bunch scallions (white and green parts), chopped

2 tablespoons chopped parsley

Heat the oil in a large skillet over high heat. When the oil is hot, add the pork and chicken livers and cook, stirring, until browned. Add the salt, black pepper, and chili powder and stir often, but resist the impulse to stir constantly: You want the meat to stick to the pan and get crusty. Add ¼ cup of the chicken broth and cook until it has evaporated, allowing the meat mixture to get browned and crusty and stick to the pan once again. Add the onion, celery, garlic, jalapeño, and oregano and cook, stirring, until the vegetables are nicely browned and crusty and beginning to stick to the pan. Add the rice, the remaining 1¼ cups broth, the scallions, and parsley. Stir until the liquid is absorbed and the rice is heated through.

NOTE: When making dishes that involve rice, remember that your flavor base will seem overly seasoned until the rice absorbs the flavors. In Cajun cooking, salt is the most crucial ingredient to get right, so you'll want to taste the dish after the rice cooks and adjust accordingly.

# Oyster and Cornbread Stuffing

SERVES 12 OR MORE

I make a pretty good oyster stuffing, but I have to confess that I like my mother-in-law Cathy's even better. It has a certain Mom-like goodness that makes it particularly special.

I talked with a lot of relatives about how they make their stuffing, and I got some really good ideas. Their recipes all had a few key details in common. They all contain some sort of meat, whether it's oysters, bacon, liver, chicken, or boiled turkey meat. They all include sage, and they all add some kind of stock to make the dressing moist.

In this recipe, briny oysters and smoky bacon create an intriguing layer of flavor that melds beautifully with the earthy, rich flavor of chicken livers.

For the best results, make the Crusty Cornbread a day in advance so it has time to dry out a bit. Be sure to save the vegetable scraps (including onion peels, pepper stems and ribs, and celery trimmings) from the stuffing prep, as you can use them to make a more flavorful turkey stock. This is another one of those dishes that is very difficult to stop eating.

Turkey stock
1 turkey neck, cut into 2-inch pieces
1 cup turkey or chicken gizzards
    or livers
5 bay leaves
4 cups chicken broth or water

2 tablespoons vegetable oil
1 medium onion, finely chopped
3 celery stalks, finely chopped
1 medium green bell pepper, cored,
    seeded, and finely chopped

½ recipe Crusty Cornbread (page 173),
    crumbled finely
3 large eggs, lightly beaten
2 cups shucked oysters, cut into thirds
1 bunch scallions (green and white parts),
    coarsely chopped
½ bunch flat-leaf parsley, coarsely
    chopped (about ½ cup)
2½ teaspoons salt
1½ teaspoons ground black pepper
1½ teaspoons poultry seasoning
¼ teaspoon dried thyme

Place the turkey neck pieces, gizzards, bay leaves, chicken broth or water, and any vegetable scraps in a large pot. Bring the mixture to a boil, reduce the heat to low, and simmer for 2 hours, until the neck pieces are very tender. Strain the stock; you should have about 3 cups. Set aside. Using your fingers, pick the meat from the neck, combine with the gizzards, and chop coarsely. Set aside.

Heat the vegetable oil in a large skillet over medium heat. Add the onion, celery, and green pepper and cook, stirring, for 5 to 8 minutes, until the vegetables begin to soften. Remove from heat and set aside.

Preheat the oven to 350°F. Grease a 9 x 12-inch baking dish with vegetable shortening.

In a large mixing bowl, combine the cornbread with the stock, the chopped turkey meat, the sautéed vegetables, the eggs, oysters, scallions, parsley, salt, pepper, poultry seasoning, and thyme. Using your hands, mix well. Transfer the mixture to the prepared baking dish, cover with foil, and bake for 1 hour. Uncover the dish and bake an additional 20 minutes, until the top is golden brown and crusty. Let the stuffing sit at least 15 minutes before serving.

NOTE: If, like me, you plan to make this stuffing on the same day you make the Smoked Bacon and Giblet Gravy (page 135), add ½ cup chicken livers, the turkey wings, and 8 cups of water to the stock, resulting in 6 cups of stock (3 cups for each recipe). You'll want to chop the giblet and liver mixture and reserve half of the meat for the gravy.

# German Festival Ham and White Bean Stew

SERVES 10 TO 12

After I sampled this rich, hearty combination at the Robert's Cove Germanfest (where it was ladled into Styrofoam bowls), it became a family favorite. There, the beans were creamy, super-thick (more like a side dish than something you'd serve in a soup bowl), and laced with an incredible smoked ham flavor. Whole-grain mustard and collards give the classic ham-and-bean combination more flavor (and a distinctive German-Southern twist). I've made this version more stewlike because I love the smoky broth that it creates.

For a creamier texture, puree a portion of the finished stew. If you don't have a blender, you can smash some of the beans the old-fashioned way by pressing them against the side of the pot with your cooking spoon. Some beans are good to leave whole and some, like black-eyed peas, are better mashed up a little. White beans are somewhere in the middle.

This recipe makes a large pot of stew, so you can invite people over or have delicious leftovers. As with all stews, it will taste even better the next day.

3 cups dried white beans (any variety)
2 tablespoons butter or bacon fat
1 large onion, diced
4 celery stalks, diced
1 medium carrot, finely chopped
5 garlic cloves, minced
1 jalapeño pepper, stemmed, seeded, and minced
5 bay leaves
2 teaspoons salt, or more to taste
1 teaspoon ground black pepper, or more to taste

¼ teaspoon cayenne pepper
2 pounds best-quality smoked ham or tasso (see Resources, page 250), cut in ½-inch dice
2 tablespoons Creole or whole-grain mustard
A 4-inch fresh rosemary sprig, minced
9 cups chicken broth
1 small bunch collard greens or kale, large stems cut out, leaves cut into 2-inch squares

Place the beans in a large pot with enough water to cover them by 4 inches. Soak the beans overnight.

Heat the butter or bacon fat in a heavy-bottomed pot over medium-high heat. Add the onion, celery, carrot, garlic, jalapeño, bay leaves, salt, pepper, and cayenne, and cook, stirring, until the vegetables have softened, about 10 minutes.

Add the ham, mustard, and rosemary, cook for 3 minutes more, stirring occasionally.

Drain and rinse the beans and add them to the pot along with the chicken broth. Bring to a boil, then reduce the heat to low and cook the stew at a simmer for 1 hour.

Add the greens and cook for 30 minutes more. Turn off heat and let sit for 20 minutes. Discard the bay leaves.

At this point you can serve the soup as is, or, to make a creamier soup with a thicker body, puree 2 cups of the stew in a blender and return to the pot. (You can also place an immersion blender in the pot and pulse for a few seconds to accomplish the same thing.) Taste for seasonings, adding more salt and pepper as desired, Serve this stew with plenty of good, crusty bread or cornbread, torn and thrown right into the bowl, or over hot steamed rice.

# Broccoli, Rice, and Cheddar Casserole

SERVES 8 TO 10 AS A SIDE DISH, 4 TO 6 AS A MAIN COURSE

Talk about a church basement classic. I admit that I don't think I've ever seen any friends or family members make this casserole without canned cream of mushroom soup. I couldn't resist taking it to another level, so I created my own creamy mushroom soup, which adds amazing depth and character and will separate this casserole from everyone else's.

As the dish cooks, the slices of onion melt into the other ingredients. I have made this dish with traditional yellow Cheddar and white Colby Cheddar from Crowley Cheese in Vermont. They both have their place, although I preferred the Colby-style Cheddar. I have seen this dish at both Christmas potluck dinners and funerals. The dish retains heat well and can be self-served, but, more important, it really gets to the soul of the eater, delivering an almost euphoric feeling.

2 heads broccoli
4 cups My Cream of Mushroom Soup
    (recipe follows)
12 ounces sharp Cheddar cheese, grated
    (white Colby Cheddar works well, too)
½ medium onion, very thinly sliced
2 cups cooked rice

1 bunch of scallions (white and green
    parts), finely chopped
Pinch of salt and pepper
¼ cup grated Parmesan cheese
1 tablespoon butter, melted
½ cup panko (Japanese bread crumbs)

Cut the broccoli into small florets (peel and chop the stems and save for another use, like the kids' lunch). Blanch the broccoli in boiling water for 1 minute, then immediately drain and shock in a bowl of ice water to stop the cooking. This will help keep the broccoli green.

Preheat the oven to 375°F. Butter an 8 x 10-inch baking dish.

Gently warm the mushroom soup in a saucepan over low heat.

Using a wooden spoon or spatula, combine the broccoli, Cheddar cheese, sliced onion, rice, scallions, salt and pepper, soup, and half the Parmesan in a large mixing bowl.

In a small bowl, combine the melted butter and bread crumbs. Transfer the broccoli-rice mix to the baking dish and spread evenly. Sprinkle the remaining Parmesan over the top and then sprinkle the bread crumbs over the cheese. Bake the casserole, uncovered, for 20 minutes. Raise the heat to 425°F and cook 5 more minutes, to brown the top if it has not browned already. The sides of the casserole should be bubbling gently.

Let the casserole stand for 10 to 15 minutes before serving.

# My Cream of Mushroom Soup

MAKES 4 CUPS

After reading countless cookbooks from local banks, churches, schools, and cherished family recipe collections, I was truly stunned to discover how many recipes call for a can of cream of mushroom soup. I have eaten plenty of these dishes, and they have all been wonderful. In fact, every Christmas my mother-in-law makes her scalloped potatoes with canned cream of mushroom soup, and plain old Cheddar cheese, and it is amazing.

My version of cream of mushroom really does not take too long to make, and it is so much better. The real secret behind the cream of mushroom soup phenomenon is the reduction of chicken broth and mushrooms. They add great depth to a dish and blend beautifully with the cream and cheese to create a super-decadent richness that can't be beat.

½ pound shiitake or cremini mushrooms, stemmed
6 tablespoons (¾ stick) butter
1 medium onion, finely chopped
2 teaspoons salt
1 teaspoon ground black pepper

1 tablespoon chopped fresh thyme, or ¼ teaspoon dried
2½ cups chicken broth
½ cup all-purpose flour
⅛ teaspoon grated nutmeg
2½ cups heavy cream

Thinly slice the mushrooms and then finely chop the slices.

Heat a medium sauté pan over high heat. Add 2 tablespoons of the butter; when it starts to foam, add the mushrooms. Cook for 5 to 8 minutes, until the mushrooms begin to take on a golden brown color and all the moisture has cooked off. (For the best flavor, it's essential to get a good sear and color on the mushrooms. If the mushrooms begin to stick to the pan a little, that's good as long as they don't turn black and burn. If the bottom of the pan starts to get too dark before you are ready for the next step, just add a little chicken broth or water and whatever is stuck will come right off the bottom of the pan.)

Add the onion, salt, pepper, and thyme and cook 5 minutes more, until the onion is soft. Add the chicken broth, bring to a boil, reduce the heat to medium, and reduce liquid by at least two-thirds over medium heat—there should only be about ¾ cup of liquid left in the pan.

Transfer the liquid to a medium saucepan. Add the remaining 4 tablespoons butter and gently stir in over medium heat until melted. Whisk in the flour and the nutmeg. Stir for 2 minutes and add the cream. Cook over low heat for 7 minutes, then let cool.

# Super Bowl Sunday Seafood Gumbo

SERVES 12 TO 16

Remember when you were a little kid and you would wake up early on Christmas morning feeling super-excited? That's how I feel on Super Bowl Sunday. I jump out of bed, start my day with a cold beer, and begin making gumbo. This particular gumbo, brimming with Louisiana bounty, is my favorite dish to make. In fact, you might say that this gumbo was the dish that made me want to become a chef. My mother always made gumbo on Super Bowl Sunday, and I started doing the same when I moved out West, going to Chinatown to shop for my ingredients.

Spare no expense for this recipe. Get the freshest seafood you can find, and plenty of it, to extract all the sweet, briny flavors. The stock is key—it should be rich and full of flavor. The roux is made with vegetable oil, not butter, because its neutral flavor really lets the seafood shine.

At least 6 cold beers for the chef
4 pounds medium (16–20 count) head-on
    shrimp
6 blue crabs
Salt

Seafood stock
1 small onion, coarsely chopped
1 celery stalk, coarsely chopped
2 garlic cloves, smashed
2 tablespoons vegetable oil
2 teaspoons paprika
1 (4-inch) fresh rosemary sprig or
    2 tablespoons dried
13 bay leaves
9 quarts water

Gumbo
1 large onion
2 medium green bell peppers
3 celery stalks

2 jalapeño peppers, stemmed, seeded, and
    finely chopped
3 cups vegetable oil
4 cups all-purpose flour
6 garlic cloves, minced
2 tablespoons salt
2½ teaspoons paprika
2 teaspoons filé powder
2 teaspoons chili powder
1½ teaspoons ground black pepper
1 teaspoon cayenne pepper
1 teaspoon white pepper
1 teaspoon dried oregano
½ teaspoons red pepper flakes
½ teaspoon dried thyme
Several dashes of hot sauce
2 pints shucked oysters, liquor strained
    and reserved
1 pound crab claw meat, carefully picked
    over for shells

Peel the shrimp and set the shells and heads aside in a bowl in the refrigerator.

Bring a large pot of salted water to a boil. Add the crabs and a generous amount of salt, cover the pot, and boil for 5 to 7 minutes. Drain immediately and set the crabs aside to

## REFLECTIONS ON MAKING ROUX

The process of making roux can be hypnotic. It takes about an hour, and you can't stop stirring or walk away from it. Watching the oil and flour mixture slowly change color and begin to take on its unique aroma gives you plenty of time to be alone with your thoughts. Once the roux has reached its proper color, the chopped vegetables are added, which creates a near volcanic reaction of bubbling, steaming, and sizzling. The roux at this point is around 400°F and the addition of cold vegetables causes an explosion of flavors and smells. Once I had to run to the store right after making roux and the lady at the checkout said, "Wow, something sure smells good."

I replied, "That would be me." She laughed and I said, "No, really, I've been making gumbo—it's me you're smelling."

"You're right," she said. "It *is* gumbo I smell."

That's how powerful the aroma is.

cool. (If you were going to fully cook the crabs, you would boil them for 10 to 15 minutes, but you want to leave most of the flavor in the crab to cook in the gumbo, so here you're cooking them just enough to take them apart.)

To make the seafood stock, put the chopped onion and celery and smashed garlic cloves in a medium mixing bowl and set aside. Peel the front flaps and tops off the crabs and place in a large bowl with the shrimp heads and shells. Use your fingers to scoop out the orange back fat from the middle of the crab and set aside in a small bowl. Break the crab bodies into four pieces and set aside for the gumbo.

Heat the oil in a large pot over high heat. Add the reserved shrimp shells and heads and the crab shells. Cook, stirring until the shells turn pink, 3 to 4 minutes. Add the coarsely chopped vegetables, paprika, rosemary, bay leaves, and 9 quarts of water and bring to a boil. Reduce the heat and simmer for 1 hour; strain.

For the gumbo vegetables, dice the onion, bell peppers, and celery. Set aside with the jalapeños to add to the roux.

To make the roux, heat the 3 cups vegetable oil in a large Dutch oven over medium-high heat. When the oil is hot but not smoking, whisk in the flour and reduce the heat to medium. Cook, whisking constantly and slowly until the roux has thickened and is the color of a dark copper penny, 45 minutes to an hour. You'll want to reduce the heat gradually as you go. When the roux first begins to take on color, for instance, reduce the heat to medium.

Continue in this fashion, gradually lowering the heat as the color of the roux deepens. By the end of the cooking, when the roux is appropriately dark, the heat should be on low. It's essential to whisk the roux constantly as it cooks (but not so vigorously that you splatter the roux and burn yourself!), because if even a small bit of flour sticks to the pot, it will become spotty, scorch quickly, and burn the entire roux.

Add the onion, bell pepper, celery, jalapeños, and the reserved crab back fat and stir until they are well coated. Stir in the garlic, salt, paprika, filé powder, chili powder, black pepper, cayenne, white pepper, oregano, red pepper flakes, thyme, and hot sauce and continue to cook, stirring, for a few minutes. Add two-thirds of the strained stock and the oyster liquor, bring the mixture to a boil, then reduce the heat and simmer, stirring frequently and scraping the bottom of the pot to ensure nothing clumps and burns, until the mixture returns to a simmer.

Start skimming the oil from the top of the gumbo almost instantly (by the end of the cooking process, the gumbo will have released almost all of the oil from the roux). Continue to simmer and skim for about 1 hour. Taste the stock. If it still has a strong roux flavor, gradually add the remaining one-third stock (if it doesn't, freeze remaining stock for another use) until the flavor tastes more like the stock than the roux.

When the flavor has developed and the stock is clearer (with fewer dots of oil), add the oysters and crab meat. Bring the gumbo back to a simmer and simmer for 15 to 20 minutes. Skim once more and add the shrimp, and simmer for 1 more hour.

NOTE: For an even richer stock, double the amount of shrimp shells, or add 3 to 4 pounds of fish bones. (If you use fish bones, add them after you toast the shrimp shells.)

Gumbo for Granny As I was flying to Louisiana from California for my granny's funeral, I wondered who was going to make gumbo, since it had always been her dish.

I guess you can say that gumbo is my dish, too, and I couldn't think of a better way to honor Granny than to be the one to make it for her funeral. I'll go so far as to say that it was the most important thing I have ever cooked. At this time, my family knew I was working as a chef, but none of them had ever tasted my food, let alone my gumbo. As I stirred the oil and flour to make the roux, I was overwhelmed with emotion. One moment I would feel extremely proud, the next moment I'd be overcome with sorrow. For me, that pot of gumbo was more than just food for the masses—this was my gift to Granny and to my entire family.

Granny usually made chicken and sausage gumbo, but my specialty is seafood gumbo full of crabs, shrimp, and oysters, simmered in a deeply flavored stock made from a very dark (nearly black) roux—not the dainty light brown seafood gumbo you see around. As my relatives devoured the soup, I got the impression that they had never seen a seafood gumbo so extravagantly filled with seafood. Their enthusiastic response was more than I could have hoped for. It's one thing to cook for my customers and to worry about what they think, but this was my first time I prepared my ancestors' food for my extended family.

Recently, I had dinner with my dad's two sisters, and they remembered fondly that pot of gumbo. I know that preparing the dish that day helped me find peace with Granny's passing.

# Fried Chicken and Andouille Gumbo

SERVES 10 TO 12

Where I grew up in Louisiana, there were only two kinds of gumbo: chicken and sausage, and seafood. I love both, of course, but this recipe in particular holds a special place because it's similar to my granny's. Unabashedly rustic, this gumbo has chicken bones and skin in the pot, two ingredients essential for depth and flavor (trust me on this, I've tried leaving them out). Frying the chicken first seasons the oil for making the roux, adding another layer of flavor.

The choice of sausage is important because the gumbo takes on its character. I use spicy andouille sausage or another smoked sausage as long as it isn't overly smoky. You can use any sausage that you like, but you'll want to adjust the seasonings accordingly (be sure to taste it before adding it to your gumbo).

1 (3- to 4-pound) chicken

Chicken seasoning
2 teaspoons salt
1 teaspoon ground black pepper
½ cup all-purpose flour

1¼ cups plus 2 tablespoons vegetable oil
1½ cups all-purpose flour
1 medium onion, cut into small dice
3 celery stalks, cut into small dice
1 poblano chile, stemmed, seeded, and cut into small dice
1 green bell pepper, cored, seeded, and cut into small dice

1 jalapeño pepper, stemmed, seeded, and finely chopped
3 garlic cloves, minced
1 tablespoon salt
1 ½ teaspoons ground black pepper
1 teaspoon cayenne pepper
1½ teaspoons chili powder
1 teaspoon ground white pepper
1 teaspoon paprika
1½ teaspoons filé powder
3 quarts chicken broth
1 pound andouille sausage, sliced into ½-inch half-moons
3 cups sliced (½-inch slices) okra (about 1 pound)

Cut the chicken into eight pieces with the skin on. Cut the breast meat from the bones and chop into 2-inch pieces. Lay the chicken on a plate or sheet pan and season evenly on both sides with salt and pepper. Dust with flour and shake off excess.

Heat 1¼ cups of the oil in a large cast-iron skillet to 350°F over medium-high heat (a pinch of flour should sizzle in the oil when it's ready). Fry the chicken in batches so as not to overcrowd the pan, about 3 minutes on each side, until light golden (the chicken does not need to cook all the way through; it just needs to color). Transfer the chicken to a plate lined with paper towels.

Add the flour to the oil and stir gently with a whisk, preferably one with a long handle (see Note). Leave the heat on medium-high for the first 10 minutes. As the roux starts to darken, lower the heat in increments. When the roux reaches a light brown color, reduce the heat to low and continue cooking until it takes on a smooth dark brown color, about 40 minutes total.

Carefully and slowly stir the onion, celery, peppers, garlic, salt, black pepper, cayenne, chili powder, white pepper, paprika, and filé powder into the roux and stir with a wooden spoon. (Don't use the whisk because the roux will be very thick at this point.) Be careful when adding the vegetables to the roux because it will create a burst of steam. Allow the roux to cool briefly.

Transfer the roux to a large soup pot. Heat the roux over medium-high heat, stir in the chicken broth, and bring to a boil. Whisk the stock frequently as it comes to a boil because roux can stick to the bottom of the pot. Reduce heat to low and simmer for about 30 minutes. Every now and then skim off the oil that rises to the surface; a good bit will float to the top as the soup cooks.

Add the chicken and continue to simmer, stirring occasionally, for 45 minutes. Add the sausage and simmer very slowly for about 1 more hour, skimming all the while, until the chicken falls away from the bones. Taste the stock. If it still has a strong roux flavor, add a few more cups of stock or water.

Heat the remaining 2 tablespoons oil in a medium skillet over medium-high heat. Add the okra and sauté, stirring or flipping the okra in the skillet, for about 8 minutes until it's lightly browned and the gooey slime has cooked out. Add the okra to the gumbo and simmer an additional 15 minutes.

The gumbo is finished when there is no more oil rising to the top. As with all soups and stews, gumbo is always better the second day, so you'll be happy to have plenty of leftovers.

NOTE: Although you *can* stir the roux with a metal spoon, I highly discourage it. A spoon collects liquid and makes it easier to splash out of the pan and burn you. By contrast, a whisk allows the roux to pass through it and reduces the possibility of splashing, as well as getting into the sides of the pan. It's important that you whisk the entire bottom of the pan when cooking roux; if you miss a spot the flour can stick and burn, which will give the entire pot an acrid flavor. Remember to stir *slowly*—roux has been called "Cajun napalm" because, if it gets on your skin, it sticks and burns. *Roux will catch on fire if left unattended!!!*

# Simple Roasted Chicken with Lemon and Basil

SERVES 4 TO 6

There are a handful of dishes that I use to try out new cooks in my restaurant kitchens. My reasoning here is that there are certain techniques that separate really good cooks from the throngs of mediocre ones—roasting a chicken is definitely one of those tests.

A perfect roasted chicken is a deceptively simple dish. It seems so easy, but it really isn't. If you cook it at too high a temperature, too quickly, it will dry out. If the cooked chicken is sliced before it has a chance to rest, it will bleed out all of its wonderful juices.

I learned this particular method for roasting chicken from Traci des Jardin when I worked as a sous chef at her San Francisco restaurant, Jardiniere. And I have been making it at home ever since. Slipping paper-thin slices of lemon, garlic, and whole basil leaves under the skin of the chicken infuses the meat with a rich, distinct flavor. Another great thing about this method is that it's incredibly versatile. For example, if you want to make tacos out of the chicken, you could flavor it with slices of lime, cilantro sprigs, and chili powder. For an Asian-inspired meal, you could use sliced ginger, mint, and soy sauce—you get the idea.

Salty, crispy chicken skin is probably my greatest food weakness. I call for a tablespoon of salt in this recipe, but don't be afraid to use more—personally, I don't know if it's possible to oversalt chicken skin. In fact, I actually make sandwiches out of chicken skins: When the chicken comes out of the oven, peel a piece of hot skin off, peel a strip of meat off the chicken, and then roll the skin around the meat and sprinkle salt on top and snack away. Be careful not to eat the entire chicken—it's that good.

I cook this a lot at home because it's a winner with my family and it doesn't turn my kitchen upside down like some other dishes do. It's great on Sundays because it doesn't chain me to the kitchen all day. I have included a simple French-style jus (the sauce created from deglazing the roasting pan) for this chicken, which is delicious, but the roasted meat is perfectly delicious without it.

One 3½-4 pound chicken
1 small lemon
6 leaves fresh basil
2 cloves garlic, thinly sliced
1 tablespoon salt
1 teaspoon ground black pepper
1 teaspoon paprika

1 whole onion, peeled and sliced into
   ½-inch rounds
1 tablespoon extra virgin olive oil

Jus
1 cup white wine
1 cup chicken stock
1 tablespoon butter

Preheat the oven to 350°F.

Rinse the chicken in cold water and use paper towels to pat it dry.

Slice six very thin slices of lemon and put the rest inside the cavity of the chicken, along with the stems from the basil.

Lay out the basil leaves. On each one put a slice of lemon and a slice of garlic.

Generously season the chicken with the salt, pepper, and paprika. Use your hands and really massage it all over the chicken. (Don't wipe your hands yet.) Place the chicken in front of you so that the neck is pointing away and you are looking at the cavity end of it. With your index finger loosen the skin away from the chicken meat over the breast (enter right above the cavity where the skin and meat come together). Do the same to the other side. Once you have loosened the skin on each side, pick up the basil leaves one at a time and place three on each side under the skin: one toward the neck, one toward the rear on top of the breast, and one under the skin where the leg and breast meet. Try to get as much excess seasoning on your hands as you do this to work some under the skin. Now you may wash your hands off.

Arrange the sliced onions in one layer on a roasting pan.

Place the chicken breast-side up on top of the onions and drizzle the olive oil over the top of the chicken. (Having the chicken elevated slightly helps the chicken cook more evenly and the oil on top helps the skin to color evenly.)

Place the chicken in the oven and cook for 35 minutes. If the skin has not colored nicely after 35 minutes, raise the heat to 425° and let it cook an additional 10 to 15 minutes. Of all the places I have ever lived in my life, I have never had an oven that cooked at what it was supposed to cook at. In a perfectly calibrated 350° oven, the chicken should be perfect in 45 minutes.

Remove the chicken from the oven, transfer to a plate, cover with foil, and let it rest for 15 to 20 minutes; this will allow all the juices to settle.

While the chicken is resting, make the jus from the roasting pan. Start by pouring the grease into a bowl. Place the roasting pan with the onions still in it over a medium-high flame. Pour in the white wine and gently scrape the bits off the pan. When the wine has reduced by half, pour the onion-and-wine mixture into a smaller saucepan and add the chicken stock. Let this simmer for 5 minutes or until it reduces by one-third, and then pour the pan drippings back into the sauce with the butter; stir, and keep warm.

NOTE: The legs should easily pull away from the cooked chicken, although it's best to use a knife, anyway, for the neatest presentation. For the breasts, make a slice on top of the chicken on each side of the top cartilage bone. Follow the bone with your knife and the breast will come loose. Be sure to save the chicken carcass for chicken stock.

# Sunday-Night Fried Chicken

SERVES 4 TO 6

All the kids looked forward to Sunday night at the Adamses' house because that meant fried chicken. I don't really know anyone who doesn't like fried chicken; that would be right up there with not liking Elvis or football.

This recipe is really simple, but it requires attention to detail. It's important to keep the oil temperature consistent (this is where most people mess up when frying chicken). If you try to put too much chicken in the pan, you will lower the temperature of the oil and end up with greasy chicken. If the oil is too hot, you will end up with a burnt-tasting crust and a raw center.

Consider serving the warm chicken with my favorite side dishes, Perfect Mashed Potatoes (page 164) and Smoked Bacon and Giblet Gravy (page 135), and green peas with butter.

Another great thing about fried chicken is that it makes amazing leftovers and it's also great for picnics. I put sliced leftover breast meat on a soft white roll with mayo, but do consider chicken salad, a chicken BLT, chicken Parmesan. Fried chicken—it's not just for breakfast anymore.

1 (3- to 4-pound) chicken, cut into
   10 pieces (see Note)
2 teaspoons salt
1 teaspoon freshly ground black pepper
½ teaspoon cayenne pepper
¼ teaspoon ground white pepper

½ teaspoon garlic powder
5 dashes of Louisiana hot sauce
1 cup well-shaken buttermilk
3 cups lard, vegetable shortening, or
   bacon fat
3 cups all-purpose flour

Place the chicken pieces in a mixing bowl and season with the salt, pepper, cayenne, white pepper, garlic powder, and hot sauce, and toss to coat evenly. Cover with plastic and marinate for at least 1 hour, or up to 1 day in the refrigerator (the longer the better, to allow the seasonings to permeate the meat). Remove the chicken from the dry spices and transfer to a clean mixing bowl. Pour the buttermilk over the chicken.

Heat the lard in a large cast-iron skillet to 350°F, or until a pinch of flour sizzles when it is dropped in the fat.

Meanwhile, as the oil heats, remove the chicken from the buttermilk, allowing excess liquid to drip off, and transfer to a clean bowl. Add the flour and toss to coat. When the oil is ready, add the chicken pieces (shaking off any excess flour before placing in the oil), one at a time, to the skillet. Start with the larger bone-in cuts in the first round, as they will take longer to cook, and the chicken breasts in the second round (they will take about 2 minutes less on each side). For the crispiest results, it's important not to overcrowd the pan. Fry the chicken about 8 minutes on each side, using tongs to turn as necessary, making sure the oil does not get too hot (it should have a mellow sizzle, not a raging boil), or it will make the outside too dark before the inside meat is cooked. Transfer the chicken to a plate lined with paper towels to soak up the excess oil. Don't be in such a rush to eat the chicken right out of the fat; it's too hot, for one thing, and if you let it sit for a few minutes, the juices will settle and it will be more pleasurable to eat.

NOTE: Cutting the chicken into ten pieces instead of the more typical eight (two wings, two breasts, two drumsticks, two thighs) results in smaller, easy-to-hold pieces with more crispy, crusty goodness. Cut the chicken into eight pieces (or buy a pre-sectioned chicken), then cut the breast off, leaving the breast side of the wing attached. Cut the breast in half, making ten pieces, which gives you two wings, two thighs, two legs, and four pieces of breast—two with the drumstick side of the wing attached.

# Chicken Sauce Piquant

SERVES 4 TO 6

It's easy to see why this dish is a Cajun classic. One chicken will feed a lot of people when cooked this way. The word *piquant* basically means "spicy," but in Cajun cooking it also refers to a certain preparation that involves pan frying meat and making a roux. I've often heard Cajun food referred to as one-pot cooking and this is a perfect example.

If you want to save time, buy 2 boneless, skinless breasts and 4 boneless thighs.

1½ tablespoons salt
2 teaspoons ground black pepper
½ teaspoon ground white pepper
2 teaspoons cayenne pepper
2 teaspoons chili powder
1 teaspoon paprika
1 (3- to 4-pound) chicken, boned and cut into 1-inch cubes
¾ cup vegetable oil or lard
1 cup all-purpose flour
1 small onion, diced

3 celery stalks, diced
1 small poblano chile, seeded and diced
1 tablespoon finely chopped garlic
5 plum tomatoes, diced
2 cups canned tomatoes
5 cups chicken broth
1 tablespoon dried thyme
4 bay leaves
4 dashes of hot sauce
Perfect Steamed Rice (page 36)
Thinly sliced scallions, for garnish

Whisk together the salt, peppers, chili powder, and paprika in a large bowl. Add the chicken pieces and use your hands to toss until evenly coated; set aside.

Heat the oil in a large pot or Dutch oven over medium-high heat until it begins to smoke slightly. While the oil heats, toss the chicken with flour to coat.

Shaking off the excess flour from the chicken, transfer the pieces to the hot oil and fry until golden brown on all sides. Fry the chicken in two batches so you don't overcrowd the pan—the chicken should be in one layer, and not on top of each other. Reserve the leftover flour. Use a slotted spoon to transfer the chicken to a deep plate, leaving the oil in the pan.

Add the remaining flour to the oil and cook, stirring constantly, for about 5 minutes to create a medium-brown, peanut butter-colored roux. Add the onion, celery, poblano, and garlic and cook 5 minutes more. Add the chicken, tomatoes, broth, thyme, bay leaves, and hot sauce. Simmer over low heat for 45 minutes, stirring occasionally, until thickened to a light gravy and the chicken is tender enough to shred with a fork. Taste and adjust seasonings, adding more salt or hot sauce as desired. Serve over rice, garnished with scallions.

# Game Day Choucroute with Sausage, Tasso, and Duck Confit

SERVES 8 TO 10

Sausage, beer, and football—isn't life great? This dish (another favorite for Super Bowl or other party) is my take on the Alsatian classic. It would be just as fantastic (and much faster to prepare) if the sausages were the only meat in it. I like to add the duck and tasso, however, to create more layers of flavor—and simply to have several different meats to eat. I'm getting hungry just thinking about the aroma of the kraut and rich pork that exudes from this pot!

Since this dish creates a party (Super Bowl or other), create a buffet with the whole, beautiful pot, a stack of plates, and silverware, and let everyone have at it at their leisure, going up for seconds and thirds as the afternoon wears on. This dish goes really great with the wine used to prepare it or cold beer.

Duck confit is not the most readily available ingredient (or quickest to prepare), so don't feel you can't make this dish without it. This recipe calls for cutting the sausage into rounds, which makes it easier to eat with a fork (no knife required); but if you want to make use of whole sausages, feel free—you could even serve the choucroute in hot dog buns.

Another big plus for this dish is that it is exceptionally quick to put together. Once the ingredients are assembled in the pot, you simply put it in the oven and go about your day. I do recommend putting a note somewhere to remind you that it's in the oven, just in case the game distracts you.

4 duck confit legs (see Resources, page 250), at room temperature

4 tablespoons duck fat

5 ounces slab bacon, cut into ⅓-inch slices, then into 1-inch pieces

1 large onion, diced

2 teaspoons salt

1 teaspoon crushed juniper berries

½ teaspoon grated nutmeg

8 bay leaves

¾ cup Creole (or whole-grain) mustard

1 bottle Riesling (or Gewürztraminer) or other medium-dry white wine

2½ pounds sauerkraut

2 Granny Smith apples, peeled, cored, and sliced into 2-inch chunks

2 large Yukon Gold potatoes (about 1 pound), peeled and cut into 2-inch chunks

3 pounds sausage (any combination of fresh, smoked, andouille, etc.), sliced into 1-inch rounds

8 ounces tasso or other smoked ham, cut into 1-inch cubes

1 quart chicken broth

Remove the bones from the duck legs by gently twisting the bone until you can pull it out without breaking up the meat; set aside at room temperature. Preheat the oven to 300°F.

## POST-K SUPER BOWL

The Super Bowl after Hurricane Katrina was particularly special. With so many of us at the restaurant having lost our homes, we decided to carry on the tradition at the restaurant with a potluck. I cooked a huge pot of seafood gumbo. We rented a projector (for the games, of course) and turned the restaurant into our house for the night. We were all together, eating, drinking, and having fun—and that's what family gatherings are really about.

Heat the duck fat in a large Dutch oven over medium-high heat. When the fat is very hot, sear the duck legs over medium-high heat for 3 to 4 minutes on the skin side only. Using a slotted spatula, transfer the duck to a plate and set aside. Add the bacon to the same pan, reduce the heat, and render until it is not quite crisp or colored. Add the onion, salt, juniper berries, nutmeg, bay leaves, and mustard and stir to combine.

Stir the Riesling into the onion mixture, bring to a boil, reduce the heat, and simmer until the liquid reduces by half, about 10 minutes.

Stir in the sauerkraut, apples, potatoes, sausage, tasso, and chicken broth. Return the mixture to a simmer, then place the duck legs on top and gently press them into the choucroute so that the skin side is just above the surface. Cover and bake for 3 to 4 hours, until the meat and potatoes are tender and the flavors have melded.

NOTE: The cooked duck skin will dry sitting at room temperature, which will make it easier to crisp and render it in the pan.

# Old-School Chicken and Sausage Jambalaya

SERVES 6 TO 8

In my opinion, there are two types of jambalaya—Cajun and Creole. The main difference is that, in the Creole version, the rice is cooked in a tomatoey sauce, and the recipe might include shrimp along with meat and sausage.

The Cajun approach is simpler and more rustic. I prefer the way the chicken and sausage flavor blend into the rice, creating a dish with a robust meaty flavor. Searing and caramelizing the meat and onions develops colors and deeply browned flavors. Reducing the chicken broth adds that unique saltiness that you just can't achieve by adding salt. I call it the MSG effect.

Just about every funeral I've been to has had some version of this style of jambalaya, usually served in a tin roasting pan with aluminum foil on top. This dish becomes even more flavorful after it sits for a while, and it's delicious at room temperature.

Be sure to add the vegetable trimmings for the chicken broth.

1 (3½- to 4-pound) chicken, roasted
2 medium onions, 1 quartered, 1 diced small
1 tablespoon canola oil
1 pound smoked sausage, diced
2 tablespoons butter
1 green bell pepper, cored, seeded and diced
1 red bell pepper, cored, seeded and diced
2 small jalapeño peppers, seeded and minced

1 bunch scallions (white and light green parts), thinly sliced
3 celery stalks, diced
4 garlic cloves, minced
1 tablespoon Donnie's Spice Mix (page 15)
2 teaspoons salt
5 bay leaves
2 teaspoons dried oregano
2 tablespoons tomato paste
2½ cups long-grain rice, rinsed

Pick all the meat from the chicken (discard skin) and use your hands to shred it into pieces, or chop into medium pieces, as you prefer. Save all the juice and fat from the roasting pan (or container) as well and set aside; refrigerate chicken until needed.

Place the carcass, quartered onion, and vegetable trimmings into a large pot to make broth. Add 10 cups of water, bring to a boil, reduce heat, and simmer for about 1 hour. Strain the broth and discard solids. You should have about 6 cups.

Heat the oil in a medium cast-iron skillet over medium-high heat and add the sausage. Sear until the sausage starts to color. Parts of the sausage will begin to stick to the pan. When there is a good coating stuck to the pan pour in ¼ cup

chicken broth and scrape it loose. Let this cook until all the liquid has evaporated. Transfer the sausage to a plate and set aside.

Return the pan to the heat and add the butter. When it melts, add the diced onion and cook about 10 minutes, until a nice deep brown color. About halfway through the onion should start to stick to the pan; deglaze with ¼ cup chicken broth and let this reduce until the skillet is dry (or *au sec*, as they say in French kitchens). When the onion starts to stick again, add ½ cup broth; when this is almost gone, add the bell peppers, jalapeños, scallions, celery, garlic, spice mix, salt, bay leaves, oregano, and tomato paste. Cook the vegetables for 10 minutes, stirring often, until they start to stick to the skillet. Deglaze with another ¼ cup broth and reduce again until dry, then add the shredded chicken, 1 cup broth, and the juices from the chicken and reduce again by half.

Transfer the vegetable mixture to a heavy-bottomed pot and add the rice and the remaining 4 cups broth. You want this mixture to have plenty of room so the rice will cook more evenly. Cook, covered, over low heat for 40 minutes.

Remove pot from the heat and keep covered for 10 minutes more. If the rice seems unevenly cooked, leave the lid on a little longer and it will even out. When jambalaya is done, transfer to a casserole dish and serve. (If you leave it in the pot it will overcook.)

# Chicken and Dumplings

SERVES 6

Over the years, I have done countless versions of this dish, and this version is the best I've made. Cooking the chicken on the bone always adds flavor that can't be beat. Making the broth from the vegetable scraps and chicken bones, and then cooking the chicken in that liquid, intensifies the flavors or, as we say in the biz, *fortifies* the dish. Remember to cook this slowly, over low heat, so that the flavors have time to develop. Cooking this dish gently will also help the chicken keep its shape, yet make it amazingly tender and moist.

I usually use cremini mushrooms in this recipe, but I've had wonderful results with wild mushrooms. Feel free to substitute pricier mushrooms like chanterelles, morels, or porcini, if you are so inclined. The choice of wine is also important. Go for a dry white, like an un-oaked Chardonnay or Italian Pinot Grigio. Avoid whites that are fruity because they will overpower the other flavors.

Take the time to chill the dumpling batter, which helps it hold its shape in the broth. Some people sauté their onions for dumplings, but I like the raw onion taste.

Dumplings
1 cup all-purpose flour
2 teaspoons baking powder
1 teaspoon dried oregano, crumbled
¼ teaspoon cayenne pepper
Scant teaspoon ground black pepper
Scant teaspoon salt
1 large egg
½ small onion, finely minced
2 tablespoons butter, melted
½ cup whole milk

Chicken stew
½ cup all-purpose flour
1 whole chicken, cut into 8 serving pieces
1 tablespoon salt, plus more as needed

1 teaspoon ground black pepper, plus
    more as needed
¼ teaspoon cayenne pepper (or other pure
    ground chile), plus more as needed
¼ cup vegetable oil
1 small onion, chopped
1 celery stalk, chopped
1 medium carrot, chopped
1 jalapeño pepper, stemmed, seeded, and
    minced
3 garlic cloves, minced
1 tablespoon finely chopped thyme leaves
½ cup dry white wine
⅓ cup (⅔ stick) butter
2 quarts chicken broth
2 tablespoons olive oil
6 ounces cremini mushrooms, sliced

To prepare the dumplings, whisk together the flour, baking powder, oregano, cayenne, black pepper, and salt in a medium bowl. In a small bowl, whisk together the egg, onion, melted butter, and milk. Using a fork, stir wet ingredients into dry

ingredients just until blended; do not overmix. When you scoop up a spoonful of batter and turn the spoon on its side, the batter should fall *slowly* off the spoon; if it runs off the spoon, it's too soft and you need to add a few more tablespoons flour. You can use the batter immediately, but I prefer to chill it for at least 30 minutes.

While the dumplings chill, make the chicken stew. Place the flour in a large mixing bowl. Season the chicken pieces with the salt, pepper, and cayenne, then toss with the flour until evenly coated. Heat the vegetable oil in a large, deep skillet over medium-high heat. When the skillet is hot but not smoking, add the chicken (in batches if necessary, so you don't overcrowd the skillet). Reserve the remaining dredging flour. Cook the chicken until golden brown on all sides (using tongs to turn) 10 to 12 minutes.

Transfer the browned chicken to a plate as you continue to brown the remaining pieces. When the chicken is browned, pour out half the oil in the pan and discard. Add the onion, celery, carrot, jalapeño, garlic, and thyme to the skillet, and season generously with salt, pepper, and a pinch of cayenne. Cook, stirring, until the vegetables are tender, about 8 minutes. Add the wine, wait 20 seconds, and then add the butter and cook, stirring, until it melts, making a buttery base to receive the remaining dredging flour. Add the flour and stir until the vegetables are evenly coated. Add the chicken broth to the vegetables, stir gently, and bring to a simmer.

Heat 1 tablespoon of the olive oil in a separate medium skillet over medium-high heat. When the skillet is hot but not smoking, sauté half the mushrooms until crisp and browned, 4 to 5 minutes. Add the cooked mushrooms to the vegetable mixture and repeat the process with the remaining oil and mushrooms.

Add the chicken to the stew and simmer for about 1 hour and 15 minutes (skimming the excess fat from the top of the cooking liquid) until the chicken is fork-tender but before it is falling off the bones.

Preheat the oven to 450°F.

Transfer the stew to a large ovenproof skillet or Dutch oven and return to a simmer over medium heat. Use a tablespoon to scoop ovals of the dumpling batter, using another spoon to gently scrap the batter off the first spoon, onto the stew. Transfer the skillet to the oven and bake until the dumplings are lightly golden (but not overly dry), about 20 minutes. Allow the stew to cool slightly, then serve in shallow bowls.

# Pineapple-Glazed Ham

SERVES 10 TO 12

An old-fashioned glazed ham is one of the most common offerings at any post-funeral feast. (I remember going to one funeral that had five on the table!) Ham is fairly simple to prepare, everyone loves it, and it feeds a crowd with plenty of leftovers.

When it comes to leftovers, the possibilities are endless. Consider one of the ultimate comfort meals—ham and mayo sandwich on white bread. All it needs is some Zapp's potato chips and a Barq's root beer. You can mix diced ham into egg or potato salad. To be honest, though, the flavor of a glazed ham is so appealing that I usually just eat the slices unadorned, standing in front of the open refrigerator while Amanda yells at me to shut the door.

This glaze combines fresh pineapple and warm, aromatic spices—cloves, allspice, and star anise—that go beautifully with pork. If you have time for a bigger project, consider brining a fresh ham (see page 133).

| | |
|---|---|
| 20 whole cloves | Zest and juice of ½ lemon |
| 15 allspice berries | 1 cup water |
| 3 star anise | 1 fresh pineapple |
| 1 cup brown sugar | 1 (8- to 10-pound) boiled ham |

Grind the cloves, allspice berries, and star anise in a coffee grinder or mortar and pestle until finely ground. Combine the brown sugar, lemon zest and juice, and ground spices with the water in a large pot; bring to a simmer over low heat. Meanwhile, peel and dice the pineapple by cutting the rind off and slicing around the core. Cut the flesh into 1-inch pieces and add to the sugar-spice mix. Bring to a boil, reduce the heat, and simmer for 30 minutes. Allow the mixture to cool and then puree.

Preheat the oven to 350°F.

Score the ham by making ½-inch-deep cuts into the fat side, first horizontally and then vertically. Place the ham on a glazing rack on a sheet pan and bake for approximately 2 hours; the ham is already cooked, so you just want to get the center of the ham warm, 140° to 150°F on a meat thermometer.

After about 15 minutes, use a pastry brush to apply a generous amount of glaze to the ham. Repeat every 20 minutes or so, saving a little glaze for the final coating when the ham comes out of the oven.

For the juiciest results, allow the baked ham to rest for 20 to 30 minutes before slicing, to allow the juices to settle.

# Brined Fresh Ham

SERVES 12 TO 14

Brining a fresh ham in an aromatic liquid infuses the meat with incredible flavor, eliminating the need for a glaze or other embellishments. At the restaurant, I store the brining ham in the walk-in cooler. At home, if you don't have room in your refrigerator, you can place the pot or bucket in a large ice chest, and pack ice around it, as you would a keg of beer. Cover the container tightly with a lid or plastic wrap.

2 gallons water
1 cup sugar
1 cup salt
3 star anise
¼ cup allspice berries
2 tablespoons juniper berries

½ cup black peppercorns
1 sprig of sage
1 bunch of fresh thyme
5 garlic cloves
6 bay leaves
1 (5- to 8-pound) boneless picnic ham

Combine all the ingredients except the ham in a large pot and bring to a boil. Remove from the heat and allow the mixture to cool completely. Place the ham in a container large enough to hold the ham when it is submerged in the brining liquid, such as a large pot or plastic bucket. Pour brine over ham and brine the ham for 2 or 3 days.

Preheat the oven to 350°F.

Drain and cook the fresh ham for 3 hours, or until it reaches an internal temperature of 170°F.

## Food and Funerals

The real importance of food at Cajun funerals is that it brings people together and offers a respite from oppressive grieving. A Catholic wake can seem to go on forever, and people get hungry. At Hixon Funeral Home in Sulphur, there is a small room where people can leave food, and it's outfitted with a giant percolator and one small microwave. Most of the cakes and casseroles go to the grieving family's house, where everyone will end up after the funeral, but some dishes also get dropped off at the funeral home.

Most people gravitate to the refuge of the break room at some point during the wake. The room is stark and plain, with cold metal folding chairs and glaring fluorescent lights, but as people gather, it soon transforms into a special place. After praying the rosary, whispering, and being sad, it's time to get some food. The room is a sanctuary from what's happening on the other side of the door, a place to talk about the good times, to catch up with family members you haven't seen in years (or in some cases, met at all), and of course, to eat.

At Granny's funeral, I was seeing most of my relatives for the first time as an adult. Eventually, the elders began to tell stories about the Link boys and what hooligans they were when they were kids. I learned a lot about my family that day. In between bites of boudin and baked ham, we caught up and talked about our families, and looked around the room and saw the cycle of life right before us.

# Smoked Bacon and Giblet Gravy

MAKES ABOUT 4 CUPS

All modesty aside, this is the greatest gravy in the world—and the center of our Thanksgiving universe. In fact, the turkey is only an excuse to have something to put this gravy on. It is rich, decadent, and deeply flavored—everything that gravy should be.

The first time my sister saw me adding livers and gizzards to the gravy she almost refused to taste it. When she did, though, she loved it and realized their importance, which is less about flavor and more about balance.

½ cup chicken livers
1 turkey gizzard
1 turkey neck
4 fresh thyme sprigs
6 bay leaves
2 garlic cloves
6 cups chicken stock or water
2 strips thick-sliced bacon, sliced
   crosswise into ¼-inch pieces

4 tablespoons (½ stick) butter
⅓ cup all-purpose flour
1 small onion, finely chopped
1 teaspoon dried oregano
¼ teaspoon ground black pepper
Drippings and pan juices from a roasted
   turkey or chicken
1 teaspoon salt, or more to taste
Juice of ½ lemon (optional)

Combine the livers, gizzard, neck, thyme, bay leaves, garlic, and stock or water in a large pot and bring to a boil over medium-high heat. Reduce the heat and simmer for about 2 hours. Strain the stock (you should have 4 to 5 cups) and let the meat cool, then pick the meat from the wings and neck, chop finely, and set aside.

Render the bacon in a large skillet over medium heat until it releases its fat. Using a slotted spoon, transfer the bacon to a separate plate, leaving the fat in the skillet. Add the butter to the pan, and when it melts, add the flour. Stir over medium-low heat until it forms a medium-brown peanut butter–colored roux.

Add the onion, oregano, pepper, reserved bacon, and chopped meat mixture and cook, stirring, until the ingredients are coated with the roux, about 3 minutes. Stir in 4 cups of the reserved stock and simmer slowly, stirring occasionally, for 20 to 30 minutes, until the flavors have melded and the consistency is thick enough to coat the back of the spoon. To finish the gravy, stir in the degreased pan drippings from the turkey (or chicken). Taste for seasonings, adding salt as desired.

NOTE: I like to finish my sauces, including this gravy, with a squeeze of fresh lemon juice just before serving to brighten up the flavors.

# Boudin-Stuffed Turkey Breast

SERVES 12 TO 15

One year at Thanksgiving, I invited fifteen people over for dinner, forgetting the fact that Amanda and I had only *one* oven big enough for *one* turkey. I came up with this recipe as a way to cook another bird outside on the grill, boning out a breast, lightly pounding it, and rolling it around a boudin stuffing. It was a huge hit, and this dish is now a Thanksgiving tradition that rivals the roasted bird.

As the rich boudin mixture cooks slowly in the middle of the breast, seasoning the turkey from the inside, the gentle heat and smoke season the turkey from the outside, resulting in an incredible flavor and texture. When sliced, the stuffed breast makes a dramatic presentation, with its golden crust and swirls of meaty, salty boudin through the middle.

I've cooked this turkey on two types of grills. The first time was a basic kettle grill, using the indirect heat method. I've since bought a grill that has a small "sidecar" compartment for coals, which creates a radiant, indirect heat that cooks the turkey perfectly with the right amount of smoke.

| | |
|---|---|
| 1 (4-pound) turkey breast, with the skin on | Seasoning and marinade |
| 2 teaspoons salt | 1 tablespoon salt |
| 1 teaspoon ground black pepper | 1 teaspoon ground black pepper |
| 1 pound boudin, removed from casing (about 3 cups; see page 30) | 3 tablespoons olive oil |
| 3 to 4 feet of kitchen twine | 1 bunch of fresh thyme |
| | 1 bunch of fresh sage |
| | 2 garlic cloves, thinly sliced |
| | 1 lemon, thinly sliced |

Place the turkey breast on a large cutting board or counter, skin side down. Attached to the breast meat are the "tenders"; use your fingers to move these to the outside of the breast, then make a ¾-inch-deep slice down the middle of each breast. Cover the meat with plastic wrap and use the smooth side of a meat mallet or a small skillet to gently pound the meat to an even thickness of 1 to 1½ inches (it's more important that the breast be even than extremely thin).

Season the meat with salt and pepper. Smear the boudin filling in the middle of the breast, leaving a 3-inch border around the outside edges. Neatly roll the turkey into a snug cylinder, and place it on the cutting board, skin side up. Truss the turkey with kitchen twine (see Sidebar).

Season the outside of the roll with the salt and pepper. Place the breast in a baking pan and coat the roll with the olive oil, thyme, sage, garlic, and lemon slices. Refrigerate, covered, for 2 hours or overnight.

When you're ready to cook, light the coals in the grill and let them burn until they have white edges. If you're using a kettle grill, move these coals to one side and place turkey on the opposite side. If you have a side compartment, start your coals in there and place the turkey on the main grill closest to the side compartment. Cook for about 1 hour and 20 minutes with the lid closed. Every 20 minutes, place a handful of soaked wood chips directly on the coals and rotate the turkey roll one-quarter around so that it colors evenly. The turkey will be ready when it has a nice color and the internal temperature is 160°F.

Cover the turkey with foil and let rest for 20 minutes, then remove the string, cut into 1½-inch-thick slices, and serve.

## TRUSSING A TURKEY BREAST

Place the stuffed turkey breast on a cutting board with the narrow end of the roulade pointing away from you. Cut a 3- to 4-foot length of kitchen twine and tie one end of the string around the top end of the turkey. With your right hand, grab the string about 10 inches from the knot and hold it at a 45° angle. Place your left hand on top of the string in between your right hand and the knot at the top of the meat. Wrap the string over your left hand, with your left thumb spread out from your fingers, and make a circle with the string. Cross it over the string and go over the roulade from the top and pull it to 2 inches below the original knot, then firmly pull up the end of the string in your right hand. Repeat this step all the way down the meat; when you get to the end, turn the meat over and weave the string through the string underneath and tie another knot. Trust me, it's easier than it sounds!

# Christmas Duck
# with Orange Gastrique

SERVES 4 TO 6

When it comes to holiday meals, I tend to stay true to my childhood favorites, but it's also nice to develop new traditions for my kids. The idea of serving a Christmas goose appealed to me, but I wasn't sure it would be well received by my family, so I decided to go with duck, one of my all-time favorite meats. This recipe is basically my version of the classic French *duck à l'orange*. Classics become classic for a reason—the orange *gastrique* (a French sauce that typically combines vinegar and sugar) imparts a sweetness and acidity that is the perfect balance for the rich meat. Truth be told, I think I like the crisp, salty, fatty duck skin even more than the meat.

This duck goes beautifully with an entire holiday menu, such as Perfect Mashed Potatoes (page 164) and Traditional Green Bean Casserole (page 155), and it's also amazing with Lake Charles Dirty Rice (page 101). Duck does wonders for wine pairings, my favorite being a good Châteauneuf-du-Pape or a nice French burgundy.

| | |
|---|---|
| 1 (4- to 5-pound) duckling | Orange Gastrique |
| Salt | ¼ cup sugar |
| Freshly ground black pepper | ¼ cup water |
| 3 oranges, 1 quartered, 1 cut into ½-inch slices, 1 thinly sliced | Finely grated zest of 1 orange |
| | Juice of 3 oranges (a scant cup) |
| 1 bunch fresh thyme | Juice of 1 lemon |
| | 5 cups chicken broth |

Preheat the oven to 300°F.

Rinse the duck and pat dry with paper towels. Generously season the duck skin and inside cavity with salt and pepper, then stuff the cavity with the orange quarters and half the thyme branches. Spread the thick orange slices on the bottom of a roasting pan and place the duck on top, breast side up. Roast for 45 minutes, basting every 15 minutes. Raise the heat to 400°F and roast for an additional 15 minutes, until the skin is deeply browned. Remove from the heat and rest at least 15 minutes.

While the duck is roasting, make the Orange Gastrique. Heat the sugar and water in a medium saucepan over medium-high heat. Bring to a boil, reduce the heat to medium, and simmer until the syrup is lightly caramelized, about the color of a candied apple. Add the citrus zest and juices and continue to simmer until the mixture reduces by half into a sticky syrup. Stir in 4 cups of broth and continue to

## CARVING DUCK

Place the duck on a cutting board. Disjoint and remove a leg and thigh from the side nearest you. Use a knife to remove the wings (they will come off easily). Slicing along the breastbone, gently remove the breast in one piece. Slice the breast on the slant to make nice medallions. Repeat with the other side.

simmer until the sauce is thick enough to coat the back of a spoon (you will have 1 cup or less), about 15 minutes. Remove the sauce from heat and cover to keep warm.

Transfer the duck to a serving platter and place its roasting pan over the burners on the stove, over medium heat. Pour the remaining 1 cup broth into the pan and stir, scraping up any browned bits, and simmer until reduced by half. Pour the pan juices into the Orange Gastrique and bring to a simmer; skim off any fat that rises to the top.

Carve the duck (see Sidebar) and serve on a platter, smothered with the Orange Gastrique and garnished with remaining thyme sprigs and then orange slices.

# Post-K Meatloaf

SERVES 4 TO 6

My sous chef at Herbsaint, Kelly Hartman, developed this recipe for our post-Katrina menu. Herbsaint was one of the first restaurants to open after Katrina, and in those crazy, tumultuous days we weren't sure if anyone would ever come to the restaurant again. We decided that if there weren't any customers, we'd simply make meatloaf and sandwiches to feed the workers and military. The first day we opened, however, a lot of locals returned to town—and they were starved for a normal restaurant experience. Since comfort foods were particularly appealing at that time, we kept the meatloaf on the menu, and it was so popular that it has been there ever since. I call this Post-K Meatloaf because after these memorable Katrina days in New Orleans, all events are classified as Pre-K or Post-K.

It may seem unusual to cook the base for the meatloaf separately, but this step is essential for the bacon to mix with the other seasonings and vegetables to permeate the meat with a rich, smoky flavor.

| Flavoring base | Meatloaf |
|---|---|
| 2 tablespoons vegetable oil | 2 pounds ground chuck |
| ¾ cup diced bacon (about 4 or 5 slices) | 2 eggs |
| 1 medium onion, diced small | 1 egg yolk |
| 2 celery stalks, diced small | 1½ cups bread crumbs |
| 1 small carrot, diced small | 1 teaspoon minced garlic |
| 3 tablespoons Worcestershire sauce | 2 tablespoons Worcestershire sauce |
| 2 tablespoons brown sugar, packed | 1 tablespoon salt |
| ½ cup ketchup | 1 teaspoon ground black pepper |
| 1 teaspoon ground black pepper | |
| 1 teaspoon ground white pepper | |
| 1 teaspoon red pepper flakes | |
| 1 tablespoon salt | |

Heat the oil in a large skillet over medium-high heat. When the skillet is hot, add the bacon and cook, stirring, until most of the fat is rendered and the bacon is halfway cooked, about 5 minutes. Add the onion, celery, and carrot and cook, stirring, until the vegetables are soft, about 10 minutes. Add the Worcestershire, brown sugar, ketchup, black and white pepper, red pepper flakes, and salt and simmer for an additional 5 to 10 minutes, until the mixture is slightly thickened. Allow the mixture to cool to room temperature.

Preheat the oven to 375°F. Butter two 8 x 12-inch loaf pans or a baking sheet.
Using your hands or a rubber spatula, mix the meatloaf ingredients in a large
mixing bowl. Stir in the cooled flavor base. Form the meat into two loaves in the
loaf pans or free-form on a baking sheet. If you decide to free-form the loaf, shape it
about 4 inches by 4 inches wide. Cover with aluminum foil and bake for 60 minutes,
or until the loaf reaches an internal temperature of 150°. Remove the foil and bake
an additional 30 minutes, or until a light crust forms on top.

# Uncle Robert's Smoked Brisket

SERVES 8 TO 10

The churches of southern Louisiana are very active in providing meals for displaced families, and a lot of great home cooks like my uncle Robert volunteer their time to prepare that food. Uncle Robert does most of his cooking on a pit grill, but his grill is not the backyard variety—it's actually on a trailer, so it can travel around to different locations.

According to Uncle Robert, who takes his meat smoking *very* seriously, it's best to start your heat around 350°F on the smoker or grill for 30 to 45 minutes, and then lower your heat to 250°F for the remainder of the cooking process. About a third of the way through the cooking he wraps the beef in aluminum foil to keep it from drying out. The result is fantastic—a beautiful crusty outside and a moist, tender inside.

However, unless you have several hours to watch the grill and control flare-ups and temperature fluctuations, you will get much more consistent results by finishing the meat in the oven, which is how I do it at my restaurants. Finishing the beef in a foil-wrapped container holds in the flavorful juices and bastes the meat as it cooks.

There are several ways to smoke meat. My grill has a smaller grid (side car) attached to it with a hole in between, which allows me to keep the fire farther from the meat so it smokes and cooks slowly without drying out. The wood chips also go on this side. The stand-up smokers will also work very well. The main goals in smoking are that you maintain a consistently low temperature and that you have a means for keeping your wood chips smoking evenly.

Over the years, I've tried several complex marinades for brisket, and this simple blend of seasonings is my favorite. Using too many seasonings and sauces takes away from the pure beef flavor that comes from slow-smoking brisket.

Brisket marinade
3 tablespoons salt
1½ teaspoon ground black pepper
2 tablespoons chopped fresh thyme
1 teaspoon minced garlic

6 bay leaves
4 tablespoons extra-virgin olive oil
1 (4-pound) beef brisket
Wood chips, soaked

In a small bowl, combine the salt, pepper, thyme, garlic, bay leaves, and olive oil. Place the brisket in a glass baking dish. Using your hands, rub the marinade all over the brisket until it's evenly coated; cover with plastic and refrigerate for at least 12 hours.

About 30 minutes before cooking the brisket, remove it from the fridge and allow it to come to room temperature. Heat a smoker or grill to 300°F and place the brisket on the rack. Add a handful of soaked wood chips to the coals, periodically, to smoke the brisket (whenever the chips stop smoking, add more). The goal for the first hour is to get some color on the outside of the brisket while infusing the meat with a smoky flavor.

Resist the urge to check on the meat every 5 minutes; it's best to keep the lid closed as much as possible to trap the smoke inside. But if the inside of the grill gets too hot, open it periodically to lower the temperature or make a smaller bed of coals. After approximately 1 hour, transfer the brisket to a foil-covered pan and finish in a 300°F oven for an additional 5 hours, flipping the brisket over every hour until the meat is tender enough to cut with the side of a fork.

Grandad Adams For as long as I can remember, I could hardly wait to get to dinner at Grandad's house—I went there just about every week. Going to his and Grandma's house was always an adventure, and a family reunion of sorts; there might be up to twenty-five people crammed into their tiny house for dinner. Their kitchen was always a disaster, with piles of dirty dishes and heaps of food trimmings covering the counters, and countless pots on the stove.

My mother grew up poor and hard. Her sister, my aunt Sally, remembers the morning they had store-bought cereal for the first time; they thought they had won the lottery. I grew up hearing stories about how my mother shared one room with ten other siblings, and how she had to fight off everyone to get the food she did have. As a result, I learned early on not to turn down anything that I was lucky enough to be served, especially anything served by Grandad.

Archie and Beth Adams moved to Sulphur, Louisiana, from southern Alabama with their eleven kids in tow because they were seeking a quieter, more rural life. In his younger days, my grandad was no saint. He had been married once before (the two oldest kids were from his previous marriage). He had worked as a shipbuilder in Mobile, and then as a police officer, where he was assigned to clean up the rougher neighborhoods.

They cooked round-the-clock, out of necessity. Feeding their children, and then their grandchildren, was no small task. Those meals, and in particular Grandad's style of cooking, left an indelible mark on me. I started out eating at the kids' table, but my cousin John and I were the oldest grandkids, so our stay there was brief. We had to make way for the other thirty kids coming along, so it wasn't long before I was cooking and eating with the grown-ups.

I couldn't wait to see the bounty that Grandad brought back from Toledo Bend, the lake an hour north of Sulphur where he had a cabin, a garden, and his catfish lines (strings that held either several hooks or a cage trap, and were tied to a tree or a gallon milk jug that floated in the water). One of my favorite memories is of the time he brought home the giant catfish. I saw the ice chest under the carport as soon as we drove up to the house. Grandad took me right out to open the cooler and revealed a 3-foot catfish thrashing around in the water. When I cautiously bent down to get a better look at the biggest fish I had ever seen, Grandad goosed me—just to crack himself up. You had to keep up your guard around this guy.

Other times, he returned with treasures from his garden: huge watermelons, cantaloupes, eggplants, fragrant peaches, snap peas, velvety pods of fresh lima beans, or ears of sweet corn. This local bounty was the source of some of the best meals of my life. On most afternoons, I'd find myself sitting next to him in the living room, shelling bag after bag of black-eyed peas, cream peas, and lady peas, and trimming snap beans. The rich, sultry smells of ham hocks, bacon, and beans filled the air as the afternoon light faded and a soft haze settled on the house.

Grandad always seemed to be happiest when he was fishing or cooking, and despite the fact that he cooked out of hardship and necessity, it never seemed like drudgery. I don't know if you can actually inherit culinary skills, but perhaps through osmosis I developed a similar attitude. For me, something magical happens when food is cooking—the rest of the world melts away, and nothing exists except what's in the skillet in front of you—and it talks, breathes, and lives. The sounds, aromas, textures, flavors, and the *heat* of the kitchen—even the occasional searing burn—feel good. I think Grandad must have felt the same way.

I guess this is the real reason Grandad Adams was so important to me. He was the instigator and the preeminent figure of these enormous family gatherings, the patriarch of the family, the provider. I've learned a lot in my career from other chefs, culinary school, and travel, but what I got from Grandad will always be my greatest gift. How lucky am I? I grew up eating old-country Cajun cooking, and old country Southern food. I was the first grandchild from Dad's side and second on Mom's, so I had lots of years to eat before their eventual passing.

ALL THE FIXIN'S

My favorite part of dinner at my grandparents' house was the sheer bounty of food that would be simmering, baking, and frying when we arrived. The aromas were incredible: the air always seemed to be thick with the rich smells of pork fat. On any given night, dinner might consist of chicken and dumplings, creamy lima beans stewed with pork fat, smothered collard greens, fresh black-eyed peas, and crusty cornbread with butter and homemade fruit preserves. It was almost impossible to discern the difference between what was considered an appetizer and what was a side dish or a main course. The table would be laden with fragrant casseroles and cast-iron pots, the smothered greens over cornbread just as important as the rabbit and dumplings. We always had a little of everything. The side dishes that Grandad Adams prepared were mostly passed on to him from his parents—survival skills that everyone once knew in order to feed the family. They mostly relied on inexpensive Southern staples—shell beans, greens, cornmeal, and pork fat—and they turned any meal into a feast.

To this day, no meal, holiday, or chalkboard menu is complete without a bevy of side dishes, or "fixin's," as they're called down South. For instance, my family refers to Thanksgiving as "turkey with all the fixin's," because we all look forward to the mashed potatoes, green bean casserole, and homemade rolls as much as to the turkey. The same is true for other meals; fried chicken with fixins' could mean okra and tomatoes, creamed corn, or mashed potatoes with gravy and smothered green beans.

# Garden Lettuces with Scallion-Buttermilk Dressing

MAKES ABOUT 1¼ CUPS DRESSING, ENOUGH TO SERVE 4 TO 6

A salad of tender, young lettuces and peppery radishes is part of our Sunday night dinners at home, particularly during the fall when the lettuces and radishes in our garden are at their best (in Louisiana, the mid-summer sun tends to be too intense for the delicate plants). We grow a lot of herbs, which means we dry a lot of herbs, and the just-dried varieties really permeate in this creamy dressing. Crispy bacon is a delicious addition to greens tossed with buttermilk-based dressings, but the salad will also be completely satisfying without it.

Scallion-Buttermilk Dressing
½ cup sliced scallions (both green and white parts)
½ cup well-shaken buttermilk
¼ cup sour cream
¼ cup mayonnaise
2 tablespoons red wine vinegar
1 tablespoon fresh lemon juice
1½ teaspoons garlic powder
½ teaspoon dried thyme
½ teaspoon dried basil
½ teaspoon dried oregano
1 teaspoon salt
¼ teaspoon ground black pepper
Pinch of cayenne pepper

Young lettuces
Fresh radishes, trimmed and quartered
Bacon slices, fried until crisp and crumbled (optional)

Puree the scallions in a food processor, then add the remaining dressing ingredients and pulse until smooth. Alternatively, for a rougher-textured dressing, simply whisk the ingredients together in a large mixing bowl.

Toss the dressing with the lettuces, radishes, and bacon bits, if desired.

# Cucumber, Tomato, and Herb Salad

SERVES 4

If you've ever been to Louisiana during the summer, you know it's hot, ridiculously hot, and we're not talking dry heat—it's thick, steamy, and oppressive. The sticky weather probably explains why the simple, refreshing combination of cucumber, tomatoes, and herbs is the most common summertime salad in Louisiana; this salad is more refreshing than drinking a tall glass of ice water.

The ingredients are always fresh from someone's garden, and when I prepare this at home, they're from my garden. Summer is peak season for cucumbers and tomatoes, of course, and if you can only grow two things in your yard, I urge you to plant those two vegetables. And we always keep an herb garden at home, because they provide the most bang for the buck (in terms of a plant that doesn't take up a lot of space, but flavors so many meals).

If you have any special red or white wine vinegar, this would be a good use for it. I wouldn't recommend balsamic, though—the flavor is too strong and it will overwhelm the fresh vegetable flavors.

2 fresh cucumbers, peeled or not (see Note)
2 large ripe tomatoes
½ teaspoon salt
Scant ¼ teaspoon ground black pepper
2 tablespoons red wine or apple cider vinegar

1 tablespoon extra-virgin olive oil
15 mint leaves, coarsely chopped or torn by hand
¼ cup parsley leaves
¼ cup snipped chives

Cut the cucumbers and tomatoes into ¾-inch cubes and toss with the remaining ingredients, adding more salt and pepper as desired.

NOTE: Whether or not you decide to peel the cucumbers is up to you. Sometimes the skins are soft and tender, and sometimes they aren't, depending on the variety. I personally like the skin, as long as it isn't waxed. Sometimes I peel strips of the skin in alternating stripes because it looks pretty.

# Creamed Sweet Corn

SERVES 4 TO 6

When Grandad served you a vegetable, you knew it was in season because it came from the garden and not from the store. The thing I love best about this dish is the flavor of fresh kernels. You can't predict the flavor or water content of frozen corn, so it's not a good substitute. I've heard people say, "Well, it's in season somewhere," which may work with some ingredients, but not corn.

I asked my grandmother how she made her creamed corn, and she told me to simmer the kernels in milk, then sprinkle the mixture with a little flour to make it thicker. I find that using heavy cream alone will give you the same consistency if you simmer it slowly, and it adds a richer, cleaner flavor. The jalapeños, or some other chiles (either sauce or flakes) really complement the sweet flavor. The salt is vital for spiking all the flavors.

You can trim the kernels from the cob in two ways. The easiest method is to lay the cob flat on the cutting board, pointing away from you, and then slice off the kernels one side at a time, rotating the cob onto the flat side after the first slice so it won't slip and roll away from you. The best way, though, is to hold the cob at a 45° angle, with the tip touching the cutting board, and run your knife down the cob. This method allows you to slice off more of the kernel, and scrape off as much of the milky juice as possible—essential for the fullest flavor.

Use the trimmed cobs to make a little fort around the cutting board to keep the other kernels from dancing away.

4 to 5 ears corn, shucked
2 cups heavy cream
1 red or green jalapeño pepper, stemmed
    (not seeded) and minced

4 scallions (green and white parts), minced
1 tablespoon fresh lemon juice
1 teaspoon salt
Ground black pepper

Cut the kernels off the cobs and place in a medium skillet. Add the cream, jalapeño, and scallions and cook over medium-low heat, stirring occasionally, until slightly thickened, 8 to 10 minutes. Season with lemon juice and salt and pepper to taste.

# Okra and Tomatoes

SERVES 4

I've seen countless variations on this dish. The method I have here is to really cook down the tomatoes to make a sauce while keeping the okra firm. Cooking okra requires great skill owing to the slime factor. Whenever I use okra for anything except deep-frying I sauté it in hot oil for about 5 minutes to cook out the slimy quality. Deep-frying okra achieves the same effect. At the same time, you must be careful not to overcook it because then it will revert to mush; there has to be a balance, as you still want it to taste like okra. The tomatoes in the dish play a supporting role for the okra.

The recipe calls for chicken broth, but water or vegetable broth can be used. This thick, jammy sauté is delicious alongside any roasted meat, or served atop Cheesy Spoonbread (page 165), baked grits, or Perfect Steamed Rice (page 36).

1 tablespoon bacon fat
½ medium onion, thinly sliced
1 jalapeño pepper, stemmed, seeded, and
    finely chopped
3 garlic cloves, thinly sliced
1 tablespoon tomato paste
3 plum tomatoes, diced
1 teaspoon salt
½ teaspoon ground black pepper

4 bay leaves
1 teaspoon chopped fresh rosemary
½ teaspoon red pepper flakes
2 tablespoons red wine vinegar
1⅓ cups chicken or vegetable broth
2 tablespoons olive oil
3 cups trimmed okra, cut into 1½-inch
    slices

In a medium skillet, heat the bacon fat over medium-high heat. Add the onion, jalapeño, and garlic and sauté for 2 minutes.

Add the tomato paste, tomatoes, salt, pepper, bay leaves, rosemary, red pepper flakes, and vinegar. Cook for 10 minutes, until the tomatoes start to break down and form something of a paste, then add the broth and simmer for 10 to 15 minutes longer over low heat.

Meanwhile, heat the olive oil in a large skillet over medium-high heat. Add the okra and sauté for about 5 minutes. Stir the okra into the tomato sauce, raise the heat to medium, and simmer for another 10 minutes. Taste for seasonings and adjust as desired.

# Stewed Lima Beans

SERVES 6 TO 8

I can still remember the first taste of Grandad Adams's stewed lima beans. I thought, *Oh, man, these are great.* I always wanted seconds and thirds. Grandad used fresh lima beans when they were in season, but dried make a great dish, too.

When I cook beans, I like a tall narrow pot (versus a wide shallow pot), so the beans simmer together in a more concentrated space. It's important to get the right proportion of cooking liquid to beans. I learned from Grandad that when it comes to beans, there are three major taste components to convey: onion, black pepper, and bacon. I add jalapeños as well, but I taste them before I add them to the pot because they really vary in heat. If they are not very spicy use more, and if they're fiery cut back as you like.

1 pound dried lima beans, soaked
    overnight and drained
3 ounces bacon, cut into thick slices, then
    into ½-inch rectangles
1 small onion, chopped
2 garlic cloves, thinly sliced
1 to 2 jalapeño peppers, stemmed, seeded,
    and minced

3 bay leaves
6 cups water or chicken broth, plus more
    as needed
1 tablespoon plus 1 teaspoon salt
1 teaspoon ground black pepper
1 teaspoon crushed red pepper flakes
2 dashes of Louisiana hot sauce

Heat the bacon over medium-low heat until it is somewhat browned but still moist. Add the onion, garlic, jalapeños, and bay leaves. Cook, stirring occasionally, until the vegetables are softened and coated with bacon fat, about 5 minutes.

Add the lima beans and water or broth and bring to a boil. Reduce the heat and simmer, partially covered, over a very low heat, stirring occasionally, until the beans are tender, about 45 minutes (this time will vary depending on how fresh the dried beans are). Add additional water if the beans get too dry (they should be covered by about ½ inch liquid). When the beans are tender and creamy, remove the bay leaves and season with the salt, pepper, red pepper flakes, and hot sauce.

# Green Beans with Bacon and Onion

SERVES 6 TO 8

This was Grandad's standard method for cooking shell beans—black-eyed peas, cream peas, purple hull beans—as well as green beans. I use this method for Asian long beans (after I trim them into 4- to 6-inch lengths). Don't worry if you don't have chicken broth; the bacon and aromatics add plenty of flavor, even if the beans are cooked in water.

As opposed to the French method of blanching green beans so that they retain texture and color, the Southern approach is to cook the beans until they are soft and lose their color. In return, you end up with delicious beans that have absorbed the flavors of the onion and bacon, creating a delicious juice that goes great with rice and cornbread. Be sure to season well with plenty of black pepper and/or hot pepper vinegar.

4 strips thick-sliced bacon, cut crosswise into ½-inch pieces
1 small onion, thinly sliced
2 garlic cloves, thinly sliced
2 pounds green beans, trimmed and halved, or 2 pounds fresh shell beans, shelled

4 cups chicken broth or water, plus more as needed
1 teaspoon salt, plus more as needed
Ground black pepper
Hot pepper vinegar, as desired

Heat the bacon in a large pot or Dutch oven over medium-high heat until lightly browned but still tender. Add the onion and sauté until tender, 6 to 8 minutes. Add the garlic and sauté a few more minutes.

Add the green beans and enough broth or water to just cover, bring to a boil, reduce the heat to low, and simmer, covered, for 25 to 35 minutes (35 to 45 minutes for shell beans), until the beans are very tender and have melted into the cooking liquid. Season the beans generously with salt, pepper, and hot pepper vinegar.

## COOKING WITH BACON

As a general rule of thumb, when rendering bacon for seasoning, cut it into *lardons*, or thick rectangular cubes (½ inch by 1½ inches), and render over medium heat until it's cooked to the halfway point (the exterior should be slightly browned, but the inside will still be soft and moist). You want the bacon to still look fatty so that when it simmers with the greens, or whatever else you are using, it will still be releasing its flavor.

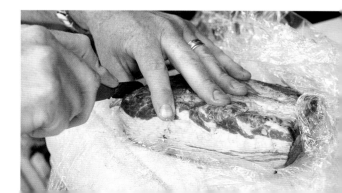

# Traditional Green Bean Casserole

SERVES 8 TO 10

Traditionally this recipe calls for canned green beans, cream of mushroom soup, and Durkee canned fried onions. As much as I have relished that recipe over the years, I always knew that using fresh ingredients would send this classic combination over the top. The only challenge in preparing this dish is that it's hard not to eat all the crispy, salty onion rings before they make it onto the casserole. Don't season the onion slices too soon before frying or they will get watery.

1 recipe Green Beans with Bacon and
    Onion (page 154)

Fried onions
3 cups vegetable oil
1 large onion, very thinly sliced
2 teaspoons salt
¼ teaspoon ground black pepper

1 cup all-purpose flour
4 tablespoons (1½ stick) butter
1 small onion, finely chopped
Pinch of grated nutmeg
½ cup all-purpose flour
½ cup heavy cream
1½ cups grated white or yellow Cheddar
    cheese

Strain the cooking liquid from the beans and reserve (you should have about 2½ cups). Transfer the green bean mixture to a large mixing bowl.

Heat the oil in a 12-inch cast-iron skillet over medium-high heat. While the oil is heating, season the onion slices with 1 teaspoon of the salt and pepper. Place the flour in a pie plate. When the oil is very hot (about 350°F), toss one-fourth of the onions with the flour. Add them to the hot oil (shaking off the excess flour as you go). Fry until golden, about 4 to 5 minutes, then transfer to a plate lined with paper towels. Repeat with the remaining onions until all are fried.

Preheat the oven to 350°F.

Melt 2 tablespoons of the butter in a large skillet over medium-low heat. Add the chopped onion, remaining salt, and nutmeg and cook, stirring, until very soft, 6 to 8 minutes. Add the remaining 2 tablespoons butter and stir until melted. Add the flour and stir until incorporated. Stir in the cream and reserved bean cooking liquid and cook, stirring, until the sauce is thick enough to fall slowly from a spoon, 5 to 7 minutes. Stir in the cheese, then add the green beans and toss until combined. Transfer the mixture to a 9 x 13-inch baking dish and bake until the casserole is hot and bubbly around the edges, about 25 minutes. Top with the fried onions and bake an additional 20 minutes, until the onions become more deeply golden. Remove from the oven and cool slightly before serving.

# Smothered Collard Greens

SERVES 6 TO 8

This classic Southern preparation is one of my absolute favorites, and it works as well with mustard greens or kale as it does with collards—just reduce the cooking time by 10 minutes or so. Collards are still my green of choice; they have thick and sturdy leaves, so you can cook them longer and let the flavors concentrate more.

Choosing vibrant, healthy-looking greens and good-quality bacon is paramount. I prefer bacon that is not overly smoky because I don't want the dish to taste like smoke. Look for a nice streaky variety with a good fat content. Avoid greens that are past their prime—any that are yellowish, or thin and papery just won't taste good. The leaves on collard greens should tear like a succulent plant and have good moisture content. Mustard greens should be a vibrant green and should have a strong horseradish spice to them when you taste them raw. I add vinegar and sugar because they bring out the greens' natural flavor and balance the smokiness and the fat.

This dish is exceptionally delicious served over Crusty Cornbread (page 173), even if it's a couple of days old, so it can soak up the greens and the juice.

3 bunches (about 2 pounds) collards or other leafy greens
4 strips thick-sliced bacon, cut crosswise into ½-inch pieces
1 small onion, chopped
2 garlic cloves, minced
1 tablespoon salt

2 tablespoons sugar
½ teaspoon ground black pepper
Several dashes of hot sauce, plus more as needed
¼ cup cider vinegar, plus more as needed
1 cup chicken broth or water

Begin by stripping the stems from the leaves of the collards and tearing the leaves into 3-inch squares; wash the torn greens in plenty of cold water. Discard stems.

Heat the bacon in a large pot or Dutch oven over medium heat until not quite crisp or colored, about 5 minutes. Add the onion and cook for another 3 to 4 minutes. Add the garlic, salt, sugar, pepper, hot sauce, and cook an additional 2 minutes. Add the vinegar, bring to a simmer, and cook until reduced by half, 4 to 5 minutes. Add the washed greens and the broth or water and bring to a boil. Reduce the heat to low and simmer, partially covered, for 30 to 35 minutes, until the greens are very tender. If the pot appears to be drying out, add more water, as necessary, to prevent the greens from sticking. Season to taste with additional vinegar and hot sauce. Be sure to serve the greens with a generous ladle of the fragrant juices.

# Maque Choux with Fried Green Tomatoes

SERVES 4

For years my wife was a vegetarian. As a guy who has sausage in his DNA, it was only reluctantly that I started preparing more vegetable dishes. Maque choux, the classic southern Louisiana sauté of corn, peppers, and tomatoes, was one of Amanda's favorites. To make maque choux more of a meal (or, though it pains me to say it, a vegetarian entrée) I like topping it with crisp fried green tomatoes. Of course, you wouldn't hurt my feelings if you wanted to throw in some bacon or sausage.

Maque Choux
2 tablespoons butter
1 small onion, minced
1 poblano chile, seeded and minced
1 jalapeño pepper, seeded and minced
1½ teaspoons salt
½ teaspoon ground black pepper
½ teaspoon paprika
2 large ripe tomatoes, diced
3 garlic cloves, finely chopped
4 bay leaves
1 teaspoon chopped fresh thyme leaves

1½ cups water
Kernels from 6 ears of corn (3–4 cups)
7 basil leaves, torn

Fried green tomatoes
1 or 2 hard green tomatoes
Salt and pepper
2 cups all-purpose flour
1 cup buttermilk
2 cups bread crumbs
Vegetable oil, for frying

Melt the butter in a medium skillet over medium-high heat. When the butter begins to sizzle, add the onion, poblano, jalapeño, salt, pepper, and paprika. Sauté for 5 minutes, stirring, until the vegetables are softened. Add the tomatoes, garlic, bay leaves, thyme, and water, and simmer over medium-low heat for 10 minutes, until the tomatoes start to break down. Add the corn kernels and simmer, until the corn is tender, 10 to 15 minutes; stir in basil.

While the corn simmers, slice the tomatoes into ¼- to ½-inch slices and season with salt and pepper. Place the flour, buttermilk, and bread crumbs in individual shallow bowls or pie tins. One at a time, dip the tomato slices first in the flour, then in the buttermilk, and then in the bread crumbs.

Heat ½ inch of vegetable oil to 350°F in a medium cast-iron skillet. Fry the tomatoes until golden on both sides.

Spoon some maque choux onto each plate. Top with fried tomato.

# Zucchini and Rice Gratin

SERVES 6 TO 8

Zucchini and yellow squash are the gardener's most common "give away" vegetables, and I think that's because a lot of people don't really know what to do with them. Summer squash is great grilled, simmered in soups, partnered with tomato sauce, and paired with rice in a delicious gratin or casserole. I think tender, buttery summer squash is at its best when it is cooked with other ingredients, especially bacon. (Of course, I think most dishes are improved with bacon.) This recipe is a great way to use up leftover rice.

2 bacon strips, cut crosswise into
   ½-inch pieces
1 medium onion, thinly sliced
3 garlic cloves, finely chopped
2 tablespoons chopped fresh thyme
1½ teaspoons salt
½ teaspoon ground black pepper
3 or 4 medium zucchini, cut into ¾-inch
   cubes (about 2 cups)

1 cup chicken broth
½ cup cream
3 cups cooked rice
2 large eggs, lightly beaten
¾ cup unseasoned dry bread crumbs
¾ cup grated Parmesan cheese
2 tablespoons olive oil

Cook the bacon in a large, deep skillet over medium-high heat for 2 to 3 minutes, until slightly browned but still tender. Add the onion, garlic, thyme, salt, and pepper, and cook for 5 minutes, stirring occasionally. Add the zucchini and cook 5 minutes more. Add the chicken broth and cream, bring to a simmer, and cook for 10 minutes; reduce the heat if the mixture bubbles too rapidly. Remove the skillet from heat and set aside to cool for about 15 minutes.

Preheat oven to 350°F.

In a large mixing bowl, combine the cooled zucchini mixture with the rice and eggs. Scrape the mixture into a large (8 x 12-inch or 9 x 13-inch) rectangular baking dish. In a small bowl, combine the bread crumbs, Parmesan cheese, and olive oil, then sprinkle evenly over the top of the zucchini. Bake the gratin for 30 minutes or until the top is lightly golden.

NOTE: The zucchini mixture will be fairly wet when it goes into the oven, but don't worry. As the gratin bakes, the eggs will bind the mixture and the rice will absorb the extra moisture.

# Aunt Sally's Black-Eyed Peas

SERVES 6 TO 8

During our Katrina evacuation, I went to see my aunt Sally, my mom's sister, in Sulphur. It was the first time I'd seen her in a while, and it was restorative to spend time together—and to be greeted by a table laden with cornbread, fried shrimp, and black-eyed peas. Those familiar dishes, which I rarely see outside of this area, lifted my spirits. As these foods usually do in the right time and place, they made everything seem normal and safe for me, and this was definitely one of those times that I needed to feel normal and safe.

Aunt Sally's method for cooking fresh and dried beans came straight from her father, my grandad—as did my own method. As with the Stewed Lima Beans (page 153), the goal here is for the finished dish to have a creamy consistency. I love how black-eyed peas break down to create that delicious creamy sauce that pairs so well with rice and cornbread.

1 pound dried black-eyed peas, soaked overnight
2 tablespoons vegetable oil
4 ounces fatty pork (such as shoulder or boneless ribs), cut into ½-inch cubes
1½ teaspoons salt
½ teaspoon garlic salt
1 teaspoon garlic powder
1 teaspoon ground black pepper
½ teaspoon cayenne pepper
1 medium onion, minced
6 garlic cloves, sliced
2 ounces (about 4 strips) smoked bacon, cut into ½-inch cubes
7 cups water
5 bay leaves

Heat the oil in a large pot over medium-high heat. When the oil is very hot, add the pork cubes and cook until browned on all sides, 4 to 5 minutes. Add the salt, garlic salt, garlic powder, pepper, cayenne, onion, garlic, and bacon and cook, stirring, an additional 4 to 5 minutes, until the onion begins to soften and the entire mixture is coated with spices. Add the water and bay leaves, bring to a boil, then cover, reduce the heat, and simmer gently for about 1½ hours, or until the pork is tender and begins to fall apart. Drain the soaked beans and add them to the pot. Cook for 1 to 1½ hours more, until the beans begin to soften.

At this point the mixture should still be a little loose or watery. With the back of a spoon, mash some of the beans against the side of the pot. This will give the beans a creamier, thicker consistency. You can also boil them for a few minutes at full heat to evaporate some of the liquid, watching carefully to make sure they don't scorch.

Consider serving these black-eyed peas over Crusty Cornbread (page 173) or alongside grilled or fried pork chops, or simply serve them with rice (and hot sauce) as a meal of its own.

# Fully Loaded Twice-Baked Potatoes

SERVES 4 TO 8

Normally I like crisp bits of bacon in stuffed potatoes, but this recipe is so rich it doesn't need it. You won't find these potatoes on anyone's list of diet foods; it's the excessive amounts of butter, cheese, sour cream, and, of course, salt that make them so good.

As far as I'm concerned, salt is the one ingredient that can make or break any potato dish, so I go for it. If you're not like me in that regard, then use 2 teaspoons of salt instead.

4 large russet baking potatoes, well scrubbed
½ cup (1 stick) butter, at room temperature
1 tablespoon salt
1 teaspoon ground black pepper

¼ teaspoon cayenne pepper
2 scallions (white and green parts), thinly sliced
½ to ¾ cup grated Cheddar cheese
1 cup sour cream, or more as desired

Preheat the oven to 375°F.

Place the potatoes on a baking sheet and bake for 1 hour, or until they are pretty soft but not overcooked. They should feel soft when you squeeze them but not *too* soft; if they overcook they will lose their starchy goodness and taste like dry, crumbly airplane potatoes. Let them cool for about 15 minutes, until they're cool enough to handle.

Cut the potatoes in half lengthwise and use a spoon to scoop most of the flesh into a mixing bowl (leaving enough potato in the skin to form a sturdy shell). Add the butter to the mixing bowl with the warm potato pulp and stir gently with a fork until the butter melts. Add the remaining ingredients and mix together while smashing the potato pulp. I like this mixture on the rustic side, so it doesn't have to be perfectly smooth.

Gently mound the potato mixture in the shells and return the stuffed potatoes to the oven. Bake for another 15 to 20 minutes, until the tops are very lightly browned.

# Perfect Mashed Potatoes

SERVES 4 TO 6

It's hard to find anyone who doesn't like mashed potatoes when they're chock-full of butter, salt, and cream, yet still light and ethereal. They're a guilty pleasure to be sure, especially when smothered with a rich giblet gravy.

I think the most common mistakes people make in preparing mashed potatoes is to under- or overcook the potatoes, or stir them too vigorously, causing the potatoes to become gummy. The goal is to *slightly* overcook the potatoes so that they crumble when pressed with the back of a fork. The potato should look light and starchy when it crumbles, not wet and dense. When you drain the potatoes, let them sit in the colander to air-dry, and let the butter soften for a minute on the potatoes before mashing.

I love salt in my potatoes, which is why I have called for 1 tablespoon. If you want to be cautious, use only 2 teaspoons and adjust on your plate if you want more.

| | |
|---|---|
| 14 tablespoons (1¾ sticks) butter | 1 tablespoon salt |
| 4 large russet potatoes (about 2 pounds) | Scant ¼ teaspoon ground white pepper |
| ½ cup half-and-half | |

Cut the butter into ½-inch pieces and set aside so it softens and comes to room temperature.

Peel the potatoes and cut them into ¾-inch cubes. Place the potatoes in a medium pot and cover with water. Bring to a boil, reduce the heat to low, and simmer for 20 to 25 minutes, until a chunk of potato crumbles when placed on a cutting board and pressed gently with a fork.

Drain the potatoes in a colander and let them air-dry for 5 minutes until they start to appear somewhat chalky on the outside.

In a small saucepan, gently heat the half-and-half until it's just warmed through. Remove from the heat.

Return the potatoes to the same pot you cooked them in (it's warm and will not cool down the potatoes). Add the softened butter and let it sit for another minute, to further soften. Add the salt and pepper and, using a whisk, smash the potatoes in an up-and-down motion, to begin mashing them. Once the butter starts to be incorporated into the potatoes, add the half-and-half and continue to mash gently, moving the whisk side to side and around the pot. Mix only until the potatoes look smooth, and then stop (this should not be more than 20 seconds total). Serve immediately, or cover to keep warm until you are ready to serve.

# Cheesy Spoonbread

SERVES 4 TO 6 AS A SIDE DISH

Although spoonbread is a Southern staple, I did not discover it personally until later in life. What a shame—once I tasted the warm, light, and creamy dish I fell in love with it. I've heard some people refer to spoonbread as a cornbread soufflé, which is a pretty fair description. Cornbread generally makes for a good side because it absorbs the juice of what it's served with. Spoonbread does that as well, but it can be pretty luxurious on its own.

At Cochon, we serve this spoonbread alongside Okra and Tomatoes (page 152), but it is a really versatile side dish. It goes well with everything from roasted chicken and black-eyed peas to sautéed shrimp dishes. One really great way to serve this spoonbread is to let it cool, cut it into squares, then sauté the squares in butter until crisp. But that takes time and patience, which is why most people just grab a spoon and dig in.

2½ cups milk
1 cup white cornmeal
Butter for greasing, plus 1 tablespoon
3 eggs, separated
1 cup grated Cheddar cheese

1 cup chopped scallions
2 teaspoons salt
¼ teaspoon black pepper
¼ teaspoon cayenne pepper

Preheat the oven to 375°F. Butter an 8 x 12-inch baking dish.

In a medium saucepan, bring the milk to a boil over medium-high heat, then whisk in the cornmeal and the tablespoon of butter, and stir until smooth. Whisk the egg yolks in a small bowl, then temper them by stirring a small amount of the hot cornmeal mixture into the eggs, and then stirring that mixture back into the pot. Stir in the cheese, scallions, salt, pepper, and cayenne until well combined, and cook for about 2 minutes, stirring. Remove from the heat and set aside.

In the bowl of an electric mixture (or by hand), beat the egg whites to stiff peaks, and then fold them into the cornmeal mixture.

Pour the spoonbread into the prepared pan and bake, uncovered, for about 40 minutes, or until the spoonbread mixture is set. (To test for doneness, insert a toothpick or chopstick into the center of the spoonbread; if it comes out mostly clean, it's done. If there is wet batter clinging to the toothpick, bake the dish another 5 to 10 minutes. )

# Cast-Iron Hush Puppies

SERVES 4 AS A SIDE DISH

When I was attending Louisiana State University in Baton Rouge there was (and still is) a restaurant on campus called The Chimes, where you could get a bowl of shrimp and corn soup with a side of hush puppies for about five dollars, which left us enough money to get a pitcher of beer. For a poor college student, that's a pretty good deal. They were the best I'd tasted—until these. The addition of pureed "green" flavors like jalapeños, scallions, and parsley adds a fresh, bright taste and gives them a cool color, too.

½ small onion, chopped
1 small jalapeño pepper, stemmed, seeded, and chopped
1 bunch scallions (green and white parts), thinly sliced
2 tablespoons minced parsley
1 cup yellow cornmeal
½ cup all-purpose flour

1 tablespoon sugar
2½ teaspoons baking powder
½ teaspoon salt
1 teaspoon dried thyme
¼ teaspoon cayenne pepper
¾ cup whole milk
1 egg
Vegetable oil, for frying

Combine the onion, jalapeño, scallions, and parsley in a food processor or blender and pulse to a rough puree.

Whisk together the cornmeal, flour, sugar, baking powder, salt, thyme, and cayenne in a small bowl.

In a separate bowl, whisk together the milk and egg. Add the vegetable puree and stir to combine. Add the wet ingredients to the dry ingredients and stir until combined. For the best results, refrigerate the batter for at least 30 minutes before frying.

Heat 3 inches of oil in a 4- to 5-quart heavy pot (preferably cast-iron) over high heat until it reaches 350°F.

Working in batches of six, carefully add the batter to the hot oil 1 heaping tablespoon at a time; use another spoon to scrape it off, keeping it in a ball shape. Fry, turning, until golden, 2 to 3 minutes, then transfer with a slotted spoon to paper towels to drain briefly. Transfer the hush puppies to a shallow baking pan and keep hot in a 200°F oven while frying remaining batter (bring the oil back to 350°F in between batches).

# Linda Zaunbrecher's Homemade Rolls

MAKES 10 TO 12 ROLLS

We were served a version of these soft rolls in elementary school, and I still love them. I'm not alone; whenever I make them, everyone who grew up around here has similarly fond childhood memories of them. These tender rolls are absolutely the best when they're hot and buttery and straight from the oven. I got this recipe from my aunt Linda, and I use the dough, which is surprisingly simple to make, for more than just dinner rolls (it also makes great sandwich rolls, which I shape slightly flatter and longer, and even great beignets).

On a recent trip to Cajun Country, I had the honor of tasting a batch that Linda made. They were amazing—I think she brushes a little more butter on the tops of her rolls than I do.

1 package (2¼ teaspoons) active dry yeast
½ cup lukewarm water
½ cup shortening or lard
⅓ cup sugar
1 tablespoon salt

½ cup boiling water
1 egg, lightly beaten
3½ to 4 cups all-purpose flour
8 tablespoons (1 stick) butter, melted

In a small bowl, stir together the yeast and warm water. Set aside.

In a large mixing bowl, use a small whisk or fork to combine the shortening, sugar, salt, and boiling water. Allow this mixture to cool for a few minutes. (Alternatively, you can combine the ingredients in the bowl of an electric mixer. Beat for 2 minutes using the paddle attachment until combined, then cool.)

Use a fork to stir the beaten egg and yeast into the shortening mixture, then add 3 cups of the flour (add the remaining ½ to 1 cup as you knead). When the mixture pulls together into a dough and you can no longer stir it with a fork, use your hands (lightly flour them first). Lightly flour a work surface, turn the dough out, and knead until the dough has a smooth sheen and does not stick to the surface, about |5 minutes. The dough should still be soft, but not sticking to the counter or your hands.

Cover the dough and set it in a warm place to rise for 30 to 40 minutes, until it has risen by 25 to 30 percent. Punch the dough down, knead very briefly (30 seconds to a minute), shape into 2-inch rolls or squares, and let rise another 15 to 20 minutes.

Preheat the oven to 325°F.

Bake the rolls on a buttered sheet pan or in a 8 x 12-inch casserole dish for about 20 minutes, until golden brown. When you take the rolls out of the oven, brush the tops with the melted butter.

# Flaky Buttermilk Biscuits

MAKES 8 TO 10 BISCUITS

Breakfast might be my favorite meal of the day, especially when warm, flaky biscuits are involved. You'll note that I use of two kinds of fat in this recipe. The shortening gives the biscuits a light, flaky texture, and the butter adds richness and flavor. Brushing the biscuits with additional melted butter during the last few minutes of cooking adds extra goodness.

This recipe really is quick and easy—handy when you need to crank out breakfast for a crowd. Come to think of it, that's no doubt why these biscuits were always served at the Adamses' house—flour, shortening, and buttermilk are inexpensive staples that could be quickly combined to feed a big group.

Homemade fruit preserves are a fixture in most Southern kitchens, and a spoonful takes these biscuits to another level. Try them with Fig-Ginger Preserves (page 172).

2 cups all-purpose flour
1 tablespoon baking powder
Pinch of salt
¼ cup vegetable shortening

4 tablespoons (½ stick) cold butter, plus
2 tablespoons, melted
¾ cup well-shaken buttermilk

Preheat the oven to 400°F.

In a medium bowl, whisk together the flour, baking powder, and salt. Use a pastry blender or your fingers to cut the shortening and 4 tablespoons butter into the flour, until the mixture is coarse and pebbly. Using a fork, work in the buttermilk. Turn out the dough onto a lightly floured work surface. Gently knead the dough and pat into a rectangle about 1 inch thick.

Lightly dust the surface of the dough with flour. The dough should feel tacky, slightly wet and sticky to the touch, not dry.

Using your hands or a pastry scraper, fold the dough in half, then gently roll out into a 1-inch-thick rectangle again. Repeat this process twice, using a light hand with the rolling pin. Use a sharp knife to cut the dough into 8 to 10 equal squares or circles, as you prefer. (You can also cut them into larger shapes and make 4 to 6 biscuits.)

Place the biscuits on an ungreased baking sheet and bake for 25 to 30 minutes, until golden brown. The last 2 minutes of baking, brush (or drizzle) the tops of the biscuits with the melted butter.

# Fig-Ginger Preserves

MAKES FIVE 8-OUNCE JARS

Many of my friends and family in Cajun Country are lucky enough to have huge fig trees in their backyards. For two to four weeks each summer, those trees produce an unbelievable amount of fruit, so preserving is key. Many locals like to preserve their figs whole, but I like mine to be fairly broken down, so they spread better on buttermilk biscuits, toasted bread, and pound cake. A hint of ginger is a nice counterpoint to the extreme sweetness of figs.

3 pounds fresh figs
2 pounds sugar

⅓ cup ginger juice (from a 6-ounce piece of fresh ginger; see Note)
2 lemons, thinly sliced

Stem the figs and cut the fruit into small pieces. Heat the figs, sugar, ginger juice, and lemon slices in a medium saucepan over low heat for 1½ hours, stirring occasionally, until the mixture is thick and syrupy.

Sterilize five 8-ounce jars in boiling water. Fill the jars with the preserves straight from the pot and seal, then process according to jar manufacturer's instructions.

NOTE: To make ginger juice, run fresh ginger root through a juicer, or grate it and then squeeze the juice out with your hands.

# Crusty Cornbread

SERVES 6 TO 8

I have to admit that I didn't really like my grandad's cornbread the first time I tried it. It was very hard, with a somewhat bitter aftertaste, unlike the packaged cornbread mixes I was used to. I soon discovered what made this cornbread special: dense and crusty, it held its shape under smothered greens, stewed beans, or anything else with a fragrant broth, while softer-crumbed versions fell apart.

For the best and crispiest results, pour the batter into a hot cast-iron skillet. In a pinch you can use a baking pan, but cast iron always creates the best crust (and looks great on the table).

I always run a stick of butter over the hot cornbread when it comes out of the oven (allowing about 2 tablespoons of it to melt), for added flavor.

2 cups all-purpose flour
2 cups white cornmeal
2 tablespoons sugar
2 teaspoons baking powder
1 tablespoon salt
½ teaspoon ground black pepper
1 cup well-shaken buttermilk

1½ cups milk
1 large egg
6 tablespoons butter, melted, plus
    2 tablespoons for finishing cornbread
1 tablespoon rendered bacon fat, or butter,
    shortening, or vegetable oil

Preheat the oven to 400°F.

Place a 12-inch cast-iron skillet in the oven and heat for at least 30 minutes. Meanwhile, make the batter.

Whisk together the flour, cornmeal, sugar, baking powder, salt, and pepper in a large bowl. In a separate medium bowl, whisk together the buttermilk, milk, egg, and the 6 tablespoons melted butter.

Make a well in the center of the dry ingredients and pour the wet ingredients into the well. Use a fork or rubber spatula to stir together until evenly combined.

Remove the skillet from oven, add the bacon fat to the skillet, and swirl to coat. Pour the batter into the hot skillet, spread the batter evenly, and bake for 25 to 35 minutes, until lightly golden and firm and springy to the touch. Serve immediately or cool the cornbread in the skillet and serve at room temperature.

# Cornmeal Coush Coush

SERVES 6

One late night I found my dad enjoying a snack before bed: a bowl of cornbread with milk poured over the top. I said, "I didn't know you ate coush coush." He had no idea what I was referring to—it was simply something he'd been eating since childhood.

Coush coush is Louisiana's answer to grits. The recipe is cornbread, more or less (minus the eggs), fried in bacon fat, giving it a unique pork-flavored crunch that holds up well to the milk that is traditionally poured over the top. This is a true rustic, stick-to-your-ribs Cajun-style breakfast; to make even more traditional, serve it with a drizzle of cane syrup and Homemade Bacon (page 20) or Simple Pork Sausage (page 27) on the side. Serve the coush coush straight from the oven or at room temperature.

1½ cups white cornmeal
½ cup all-purpose flour
2 teaspoons baking powder
1 tablespoon sugar
1 teaspoon salt

1¼ cups milk, plus more to serve
½ cup bacon fat
Cane syrup (optional)
1 cup cooked bacon or cracklins, crumbled (optional)

Preheat the oven to 400°F.

Whisk together the cornmeal, flour, baking powder, sugar, and salt in a medium bowl. Stir in the milk until just combined.

Heat the bacon fat in a medium cast-iron skillet over medium heat. When the fat just begins to smoke, add the batter to the skillet and bake for 12 to 15 minutes, until springy and firm to the touch (or a toothpick inserted in the center comes out clean).

To serve, cut the cornbread into six wedges. Halve the wedges horizontally and place both halves in a bowl, or simply crumble each wedge into a bowl (everyone has their own way of eating it). Drizzle the coush coush with additional milk, cane syrup, and crumbled bacon or cracklins, if desired.

# Corn and Rice Calas

SERVES 2 TO 4 AS A SIDE DISH

The word *cala* generally refers to a yeasted fritter made with rice that's fried, dusted in confectioners' sugar, and served with jam for breakfast. Over the years I have experimented with several different varieties of rice fritters. I am really fond of this recipe. Although it's untraditional, the batter is lighter, so it can be griddled like a pancake (as opposed to thicker batters that need to be deep-fried). We serve these calas at Cochon with chopped fresh tomatoes tossed with a little oil and vinegar and seasoned with salt and pepper.

1 large egg, lightly beaten
Kernels from 3 ears of corn (about
    1½ cups)
½ small onion, finely chopped
3 scallions (green and white parts), thinly
    sliced
1 jalapeño pepper, stemmed, seeded, and
    finely chopped

3 tablespoons all-purpose flour
¼ teaspoon baking powder
1 cup cooked rice
1 teaspoon salt
Pinch of cayenne pepper
Pinch of ground black pepper
1 tablespoon vegetable oil or melted
    butter, plus more as needed

Combine the egg, corn, onion, scallions, and jalapeño in a medium bowl. Whisk together the flour and baking powder, then stir into the corn mixture. Fold in the rice, salt, cayenne, and black pepper and stir until combined.

Heat the vegetable oil or butter over medium heat in an iron skillet or nonstick pan. When the skillet is hot, drop the batter by the spoonful into the pan (do this in batches, as you want to leave enough space between them to flip them over). Cook the fritters for 3 to 4 minutes on each side, until they are lightly golden. Set the cooked fritters aside and cover with a dishtowel to keep warm and repeat with remaining batter, adding more oil or butter to the skillet if necessary.

# Creamy Potato Salad (for Gumbo)

SERVES 10 TO 12

A scoop of potato salad served in or alongside a bowl of hot gumbo is a Cajun Country concept. I was surprised when I discovered that a lot of New Orleanians had never heard of the combination. Personally, I keep my potato salad on the side and dunk spoonfuls of it into my gumbo as I eat. I like potato salad to be a little creamy, which is why I slightly overcook the potatoes (creamy potato salad helps soak up the juice in the gumbo). There is no pickle relish in this recipe because of the seafood in the gumbo; however, if you are making this salad for a barbecue or some other meal, stir in about 3 tablespoons.

4 pounds Yukon Gold potatoes
½ medium onion, finely chopped
2 celery stalks, finely chopped
1 bunch scallions (green and white parts), thinly sliced
½ cup mayonnaise

3 tablespoons Creole (or whole-grain) mustard
1 tablespoon red wine vinegar
1 tablespoon plus 1 teaspoon salt
1½ teaspoons paprika
1 teaspoon ground black pepper
2 tablespoons chopped fresh parsley

Peel the potatoes, cut them into medium dice, and transfer to a large pot of cold water. Bring the water to a boil, reduce the heat, and simmer the potatoes until very soft and they begin to crumble when pricked with a fork, about 20 minutes. Drain the potatoes in a colander and cool to room temperature.

Transfer the potatoes to a large mixing bowl and partially smash them with a whisk (leave some of the potatoes a little chunky). Add the onion, celery, scallions, mayonnaise, mustard, vinegar, salt, paprika, pepper, and parsley, and vigorously stir with a fork until well mixed. Taste for seasonings and add more salt as desired.

# OUTDOOR LIVING—
## LAISSEZ LES BON TEMPS ROULEZ!

Louisiana has some of the best and some of the worst weather, depending on how you look at it. Come springtime, we revel in outdoor crawfish boils, jazz fests, and the most perfect, sparkling weather of anywhere I've been. There's something wonderful about a crawfish boil in the late spring—the sensual experience of sucking heads of spicy crawfish and wiping the sweat from your brow. The summers here can be brutal, but that's when we go to the beach or up to the "camp," put on our shorts, crank up the fans, and watch the awesome show of the summer afternoon thunderstorms that you can almost set your watch to. The sweltering summers make us all the more grateful for temperate weather the rest of the year.

Most of the best festivals take place in spring and the fall, which make for great outdoor dancing and beer drinking. Maybe that's why Louisiana has so many festivals—everyone here really likes to be outside. When we get together with friends, it's always outside; there always seems to be too many of us to be in the house, anyway. Besides, all the cooking is going on outside: crawfish boils, barbecues, pig roasts.

Then there's Toledo Bend, my family's camp. My dad's place is one room that holds one bed, one couch bed, a kitchen, and the deck; the deck is where it all happens. We don't go to the camp to hang out indoors—we have breakfast, lunch, and dinner outside. The hearty, lazy breakfasts alone make the long drive from New Orleans worthwhile. Even if it's raining, we eat outside. In fact, I look forward to the outdoor breakfasts more than any other thing we do up there. I've also spent many a late night drinking wine on the deck.

I tell everyone from out of town this same thing. If you really want to experience Louisiana, pick a festival and bring your dancing shoes and get ready to eat. I'll never forget my first festival in Louisiana—it was in the middle of a field that pulsated with music, food, and dancing. The air was thick with the smell of sausage smoking, spicy étouffées, fried cracklins, boulettes, pistollettes, and so much more. I remember thinking, *How amazing is this*, a place where you can have all your favorite foods in one place and Cajun music, rides, and dancing to boot. I don't know why, but food always seems to taste better outdoors.

Since then, I have been to countless festivals across the state, from Contraband Days in Lake Charles to Jazz Fest in New Orleans, and the food is always my main motivation for going.

The recipes in this chapter are foods that I eat and cook outdoors, from handheld snacks at festivals to breakfasts and dinners that we prepare at the lake. There are also simple recipes inspired by outdoors, like pan-fried fish and grilled oysters that are simple enough to cook over a campfire (or inside if you insist).

# Natchitoches Meat Pies

MAKES ABOUT 16 PIES

In Louisiana, Natchitoches is famous for its extravagant display of Christmas lights, but it is also famous for meat pies—with good reason. The spicy seasonings and mix of chiles, onions, and beef make an unforgettable snack that's perfectly salty, spicy, and fried.

Meat pies are a quintessential festival snack; they're perfect for backyard barbecues, festivals, and parties when you have people standing around, as they don't require any silverware or plates (you can also make the dough a day or two in advance). They are really great the next day, cold for breakfast as well. Another cool thing about ground meat pies is that they can be made all year long, whereas crawfish pies are seasonal. I must warn you about these pies: You can eat more of them than your stomach can handle, and you won't realize it until it's too late, so be careful.

2 tablespoons vegetable oil
1 pound ground beef (not lean)
1 tablespoon salt
½ teaspoon cayenne pepper
1 teaspoon paprika
½ teaspoon chili powder
¼ teaspoon ground white pepper
½ teaspoon ground cumin
½ teaspoon ground black pepper
1 small onion, finely chopped
1 green bell pepper, cored, seeded, and finely chopped
1 medium jalapeño pepper, stemmed, seeded, and finely chopped

4 plum tomatoes, diced
1 teaspoon dried thyme
4 bay leaves
½ teaspoon Worcestershire sauce
2 tablespoons all-purpose flour
2 tablespoons water
1 bunch of scallion (green and white parts), thinly sliced (about ½ cup)
5 dashes Louisiana hot sauce
Meat Pie Dough (recipe follows), chilled
1 egg, lightly beaten
Vegetable oil, for frying

Heat the vegetable oil in a 12-inch cast-iron skillet over medium-high heat. Add the meat, salt, cayenne, paprika, chili powder, white pepper, cumin, and black pepper and cook, using a metal spatula to break up the meat, for 5 to 8 minutes, or until the meat is lightly browned.

Add the onion, bell pepper, jalapeño, tomatoes, dried thyme, bay leaves, and Worcestershire sauce and cook, stirring, for an additional 5 to 10 minutes, until most of the juices have evaporated and the vegetables have softened.

Dust the flour over the meat and add the water, stirring to combine (this should tighten up the mixture enough so it won't leak moisture when it's encased in the dough). Stir in the scallions and hot sauce and transfer the mixture to a baking pan (or dish) to cool for 20 minutes at room temperature and at least 15 minutes in the refrigerator.

When you're ready to prepare the pies, line two baking sheets with parchment paper and a dusting of flour. Divide the dough into four even sections to make it easier to work with. Return three of the sections to the refrigerator. Dust the counter with a sprinkling of flour and roll out the first section until it's just under ¼ inch thick. Using a 4-inch biscuit cutter (or a similar size bowl or jar lid), cut the dough into rounds. Save the scraps; they can be rerolled if needed.

Lightly brush the outer edges of each circle with beaten egg. Place 2½ table-spoons of filling in the center of each round. Fold the circle over the filling to make a half circle. Using the back side of fork tines, press around the edges to seal the pie. Transfer the pies to the prepared baking sheet. Repeat the process with the remaining dough sections.

When you fill a baking sheet, place it in the refrigerator for at least 30 minutes so the dough stays firm when you fry it. You can also freeze the uncooked pies. Just freeze them on the sheet pan first, and then when they are fully frozen, transfer them to a plastic freezer bag.

To fry the pies, heat 2½ inches of oil in a large cast-iron skillet or Dutch oven to 350°F. Fry the chilled pies in batches of four or five at a time, cooking for about 8 minutes, until golden. (Frozen pies will need 12 to 14 minutes.) Transfer the cooked pies to a sheet pan lined with paper towels or newspaper, and keep warm in a low oven while you fry the remaining pies.

## Meat Pie Dough

1 pound cold butter, cut into small pieces
5¼ cups all-purpose flour, plus extra for dusting
½ teaspoon salt
½ cup ice water
1 large egg, lightly beaten

Using a pastry blender or your fingers, cut the butter into the flour and salt until the mixture resembles coarse pebbles. Using a fork, stir in the ice water until the dough pulls together, then use your hands to knead for a few minutes until it's smooth and evenly blended. Roll the dough into a rectangle and fold it over itself three times like a letter. Repeat this process four times and reshape to a rectangle, and refrigerate until firm, at least 15 minutes.

**"The Fest"** I've been going to the New Orleans Jazz and Heritage Festival for years and have watched it grow to massive proportions—these days it's almost too big. There are multiple stages with music ranging from Cajun at the Fais Do Do stage, blues, gospel, and local New Orleans musicians, and then there are the big-name headliners, like the Allman Brothers, Lenny Kravitz, Bruce Springsteen, and so on. But the biggest draw for me is—you guessed it—the food. No other festival has more options (or cold beer). In fact, if there were an award for efficient and plentiful beer vendors, this festival would take home the gold.

Every year I do a cooking demo at "The Fest," as we call it, and then it's off to the food booths. My first stop is always the *cochon de lait* sandwich, slow-cooked and smothered with pickled cabbage. Then it's straight to the pies, as in meat and crawfish pies, and I can't help eating one of each. I can't forget crawfish Monica, a creamy pasta dish, or the andouille calas, boudin, crawfish bread, alligator sausage, boiled crawfish, and Cuban sandwiches . . . the list goes on and on. Let's just say you could go every day and not try everything.

If you find yourself at Jazz Fest, take my advice: Go early and see the music on the smaller stages, bring a blanket to sit on, get some food and beer, and grab a spot to chill. Better still, get a festival calendar and try to make one of the other festivals, especially those west of the Atchafalaya in Cajun Country. In the words of the Cajuns, *We gonna pass a good time cha. Aaaaieeee!*

# Link Family Crawfish Boil

SERVES 12 TO 16

Crawfish boils are the greatest outdoor cooking events in southern Louisiana, and they epitomize our way of life. These giant parties for adults and kids are all about having a good time, being with friends and family, and eating local food.

To boil crawfish you need to have the proper setup—namely a propane tank, a stand to put the pot on, and a very large pot (crawfish are sold in 40-pound sacks). The pot needs to be fitted with a basket so you can pull the crawfish out and add more.

My cousin Billy's crawfish are, hands down, the best I've ever tasted. When it comes to cooking crawfish, though, we aren't in total agreement. I like to soak the crawfish in their spicy cooking water; Billy doesn't. Some people prefer to drain the crawfish after they've been soaking in the spicy water for just 5 minutes, then dump them into an ice chest, and season the outside of the crawfish shells heavily. This method keeps the meat from getting overcooked, but the spices end up on your hands, not in the meat. To my mind, "marinating" the cooked crawfish in their cooking liquid allows more of the spice and salt to be absorbed by the meat and creates more juice in the heads. (Sucking the juice from the head before you eat the tail is the proper way to eat boiled crawfish.)

Though no self-respecting party in Cajun Country would cook fewer than two or three sacks, I've given a smaller recipe here.

2 pounds salt
8 medium onions, quartered
10 lemons, halved
6 heads of garlic, halved horizontally

1 (4½-pound) bag Louisiana crawfish, shrimp, and crab boil, or an equal amount of Donnie's Spice Mix (page 15)
3 pounds small red potatoes
8 ears of corn, shucked and cut into thirds
40 pounds medium crawfish

Bring a very large pot of water to a boil over high heat. Add the salt, onions, lemons, garlic, and spice mix and boil until the onions and lemon soften, about 10 minutes. Add the potatoes and boil until tender when pierced with a knife, approximately 15 minutes. Add the corn, cook an additional 10 minutes, then transfer the vegetables to a colander. Drain well, then spread the corn and potatoes on a table lined with paper. Return the water to a boil, then add the crawfish, and bring back to a boil once more. Immediately turn off the heat and allow the crawfish to soak, uncovered, in the spicy water for 20 to 30 minutes. Drain the crawfish and serve alongside the vegetables with plenty of napkins and cold beer.

## A SMALLER BOIL

Follow the directions above, using 5 pounds of crawfish, 1¼ cups salt, 1¼ cup Donnie's Spice Mix, 6 bay leaves, 3 halved lemons, and 1 pound each new potatoes and corn.

I love watching the kids chasing the live crawfish, clipping them on their shirts and having crawfish races. My most recent boil was with the extended Link family in Rayne, Louisiana. My cousin Billy Link (aka Billy Boy or Wild Bill) is a crawfish farmer. He and I went into the fields and pulled in the traps for that afternoon's boil. This was the first time I had boiled for a crawfish farmer, and the pressure was on. These guys know their stuff; even his propane burner was state of the art.

# Breaux Bridge Crawfish Pies

MAKES ABOUT 16 PIES

Crawfish pies are a weakness of mine that I associate with the crawfish festival in Breaux Bridge and the Jazz Fest in New Orleans, among others. Eating them is a family tradition, too; for years my daughter Cassidy and I have made a stop at the Cypress Knee Café at the New Orleans Audubon Zoo to eat crawfish pies and red beans and rice, our special tradition.

The filling in this pie is like an incredible étouffée packed into a crisp crust. Crawfish have a wonderful way of cooking down and permeating the other ingredients they are cooked with. In this case, the rice absorbs the flavor of the crawfish and the sauce.

I often make these crisp, fun-to-eat pies at home when I have a group of friends coming over. The pies stay hot for a long time, so they're great to set out on a plate and let people nibble on, while I finish cooking the rest of the meal (everyone's always in the kitchen). It's rare to see me without a bottle of hot sauce in my hand when I'm eating these pies—I like a dash on every bite.

2 tablespoons butter
1 medium onion, finely chopped
2 celery stalks, finely chopped
1 green bell pepper, cored, seeded, and finely chopped
1 jalapeño pepper, stemmed, seeded, and finely chopped
1 tablespoon salt
1 tablespoon dried oregano
1 teaspoon paprika
1 teaspoon chili powder
½ teaspoon dried thyme
½ teaspoon cayenne pepper
¼ teaspoon ground white pepper
¼ teaspoon ground black pepper

1 pound Louisiana crawfish meat (see Sidebar, page 56)
1 tablespoon all-purpose flour
1½ cups chicken broth
Dash of Worcestershire sauce
1 tablespoon fresh lemon juice
Dash of hot sauce
2 cups cooked rice
½ bunch scallions (green and white parts), minced
2 tablespoons chopped parsley
Meat Pie Dough (page 184)
1 egg, lightly beaten
Vegetable oil, for frying

Melt the butter in a large skillet over medium-high heat. Add the onion, celery, pepper, jalapeño, salt, oregano, paprika, chili powder, thyme, cayenne, and white and black pepper and cook, stirring, until the vegetables have softened, 5 to 6 minutes. Add the crawfish meat to the vegetables, sprinkle the mixture with the flour, and cook, stirring, until the mixture thickens, 3 to 4 minutes. Stir in the chicken broth, Worcestershire, lemon juice, and hot sauce and simmer until the mixture is slightly thickened, about 10 minutes. Stir in the rice, scallions, and parsley. Taste for seasonings and add more lemon juice or hot sauce as desired. Refrigerate the mixture for at least 15 minutes, until chilled throughout (spreading it in a shallow dish speeds the process).

When you're ready to prepare the pies, line two baking sheets with parchment paper and a dusting of flour. Divide the dough into four even sections to make it easier to work with. Return three of the sections to the refrigerator. Dust the counter with a sprinkling of flour and roll out the first section until it's just under ¼ inch thick. Using a 4-inch biscuit cutter (or a similar size bowl or jar lid), cut the dough into rounds. Save the scraps; they can be rerolled if needed.

Lightly brush the outer edges of each circle with beaten egg. Place 2½ tablespoons of filling in the center of each round. Fold the circle over the filling to make a half circle. Using the back side of fork tines, press around the edges to seal the pie. Transfer the pies to the prepared baking sheet. Repeat process with remaining dough sections. When you fill a baking sheet, place it in the refrigerator for at least 30 minutes so the dough stays firm when you go to fry it. You can also freeze the uncooked pies. Just freeze them on the sheet pan first, and then when they are fully frozen, transfer them to a plastic freezer bag.

To fry the pies, heat 2½ inches of oil in a large cast-iron skillet or Dutch oven to 350°F. Fry the chilled pies in batches of four or five at a time, cooking for about 8 minutes, until golden. (Frozen pies will need 12 to 14 minutes.) Transfer the cooked pies to a sheet pan lined with paper towels or newspaper, and keep warm in a low oven while you fry the remaining pies.

## BREAUX BRIDGE CRAWFISH FESTIVAL

If you love crawfish, you should plan a trip to the Breaux Bridge Crawfish Festival. Nowhere else in the country can you sample so many crawfish dishes in one place. You need to pace yourself for this kind of eating. I start with the crisp crawfish pies and the *boulettes*—little fried balls of crawfish stuffing—then work my way over to the *pistolettes*—a creamy, cheesy crawfish mix stuffed into small soft baguette and deep-fried (trust me on this). Then it's time to settle in for a cold beer and spicy boiled crawfish. Afterward, it's probably a good idea to dance to work off all that food, though I'd definitely avoid the rides.

# Cheesy Eggs and Boudin

SERVES 2 TO 4

In Breaux Bridge, Louisiana, there is a restaurant called Café des Amis; their famous Zydeco brunch on Saturday mornings is something that *everyone* should experience at least once in his or her life. Not only is the food great (think eggs smothered in crawfish étouffée alongside huge, fluffy biscuits), there is also a live Zydeco band playing so loud you would think you were at an outdoor festival—*and* you can order a beer with your breakfast. Needless to say, the dance floor stays packed all morning.

When I say people are dancing here, I mean they *throw down*, with full-on Cajun and Zydeco two-stepping. You can spot the folks who do this regularly by the towel or bandanna in their back pocket for wiping the sweat off their forehead. My mother taught me how to dance when I was a young boy. Dancing is a birthright in southern Louisiana, right up there with eating your first crawfish and drinking your first beer.

Des Amis is where I first had a crisp-fried boudin patty served alongside scrambled eggs; now the combination is a staple for al fresco breakfasts at the lake. I like my eggs cooked slowly and lightly, so they have a creamy texture. I can't resist stirring in some Parmesan cheese, just before the eggs set, for added richness. Consider this combination the Cajun Country breakfast of champions, especially when served with Flaky Buttermilk Biscuits (page 170) and, in honor of Des Amis, an ice-cold Abita beer.

3 tablespoons olive oil
4 extra-large eggs, lightly beaten
Salt and pepper
Freshly ground black pepper

¼ cup grated Parmesan cheese
1 pound boudin (page 30)
All-purpose flour, as needed

Heat 1 tablespoon of the oil in a medium skillet over medium-low heat. Add the eggs and a pinch of salt and pepper. When the eggs form a thin coat on the bottom of the skillet, begin to stir them in broad, gentle strokes. When the eggs are a little more than halfway cooked (when there are a few pools of liquid), stir in the Parmesan and remove from the heat.

Using your fingers, remove the boudin from its casings and form into four equal-size patties. Heat the remaining 2 tablespoons oil in a clean skillet over medium-high heat. Gently dust the tops and bottoms of the patties with flour, and sauté about 3 minutes on each side, until browned and crisp. Serve with cheesy eggs and homemade biscuits, if desired.

Toledo Bend Toledo Bend and I are about the same age, so I guess you could say we've grown up together. The man-made lake was created in 1968 by damming the Sabine River, which flooded the valley that is now Toledo Bend Reservoir. Some of my greatest childhood memories are from days at this lake and the cabin that my grandad Adams had there. Toledo Bend is where Grandad taught me how to tie my first fishing knot and where my dad showed me how to clean my first fish.

After Grandad passed, my parents bought their own place at the lake. It was quite a setup—fully equipped with a deck for crawfish boils, a pontoon boat, bass boat, and a fishing pier. When my parents divorced, years later, we sold the place, but those years were very happy times for our family.

My dad has since built his own house near the old one. It's a one-bedroom camp with a deck that's bigger than the living room because nobody really stays inside. It makes me happy that my kids are growing up going to the same lake, with my dad, their "Paw Paw," who teaches them to fish and how to drive the boat.

Toledo Bend is where our hearty camp breakfast tradition started, and for years we've cooked many of the dishes in this book. I've omitted the quickly rejected dish that my dad still talks about—soft scrambled eggs with fresh bass eggs. Let's just say he wasn't a big fan of that one. But nobody complained about the crisp fresh catfish fillets fried in bacon

fat, the eggs scrambled with boudin, or the buttermilk biscuits topped with homemade preserves.

Our days typically start predawn with a couple of hours of bass fishing, then we go back to camp and I cook breakfast. When I was a kid, my mother would always have breakfast ready when we came back (and that was before cell phones). There's nothing like the smell of bacon cooking after coming back from fishing in the morning. Later in the day, we usually have a light lunch, from leftovers, because I always cook too much for breakfast. Dinner is all about firing up the grill for sauce-slathered ribs, a succulent rib roast, and/or fresh fish, if we've been lucky enough to catch any.

There's always been something special about the flavor of the fish in this lake—a crisp, clean taste unlike any other fish I have eaten. It's hard to say which variety is my favorite; the catfish is the cleanest I've had, but you can't beat the bluegills pan-fried with a corn-meal crust. Even the water has a silver tint to it; you can see it when the light plays off the ripples the boat creates as it cuts through the water. When the white perch are biting in the spring, we go night fishing, hanging a lantern over the boat or floating car headlights in the water to attract bait, which attracts the fish. More important, it's fun to hang out on the boat at night, under the stars, and drink a few beers.

There's not too much in life these days that can make me feel like a child again, but driving up to the camp, watching the terrain change from flat to rolling hills, brings back all those memories. Then there's that first glimpse you get of the lake through the pine trees; every time I see it, it feels like the first time. The camp is our family's sanctuary. We went up to the camp a few days after Hurricane Katrina so that we could try to clear our heads. After Grandad died, I went to the camp by myself for a couple days to have a cool, quiet place to think and connect with his spirit. In the years to come, I'm sure I'll blow out of New Orleans and point the car toward Toledo Bend for no other reason than to relax with my family and prepare the dishes that satisfy and restore all of us.

# Crawfish Boulettes

MAKES ABOUT 20

*Boulettes,* or "little balls," are essentially deep-fried balls of meat or crawfish stuffing. Crispy, savory, and satisfying, they are popular at festivals throughout Louisiana, particularly the crawfish festival in Breaux Bridge. The base for this recipe is similar to that of étouffée and crawfish pie filling, but it is combined with bread crumbs (which also makes these Cajun fish patties economical). The boulettes are coated with additional bread crumbs and fried, which gives them a crisp crust and rich, satisfying flavor. Like most of my favorite snacks, these are great—you guessed it—with plenty of hot sauce and cold beer.

3 tablespoons butter
½ medium onion, finely chopped
½ green bell pepper, cored, seeded, and finely chopped
½ jalapeño pepper, stemmed, seeded, and finely chopped
1 celery stalk, finely chopped
2 teaspoons salt
1½ teaspoons dried oregano
½ teaspoon each paprika and chili powder
¼ teaspoon cayenne pepper
¼ teaspoon ground white pepper
Pinch of ground black pepper

½ pound crawfish meat (see Sidebar, page 56)
½ cup crawfish, shrimp, or chicken broth
1 tablespoon fresh lemon juice
Dash of Worcestershire sauce
Dash of hot sauce
½ cup finely chopped scallions (white and green parts)
¼ cup finely chopped parsley
4 cups dry bread crumbs
1 large egg, lightly beaten
Vegetable oil, for frying
3 cups all-purpose flour
3 cups well-shaken buttermilk (see Note)

Heat 1 tablespoon of the butter in a large skillet over medium-high heat. Add the onion, bell pepper, jalapeño, celery, salt, oregano, paprika, chili powder, cayenne, and white and black pepper and cook, stirring, until the vegetables begin to soften, 4 to 5 minutes. Add the crawfish and broth and bring to a boil. Reduce the heat to medium-low and simmer for 10 minutes, until the liquid has reduced by half. Add the remaining 2 tablespoons butter, along with the lemon juice, Worcestershire, hot sauce, scallions, and parsley and cook for an additional minute, stirring until well combined.

Transfer the mixture to a mixing bowl and cool for about 20 minutes. Add 1¼ cups of the bread crumbs and the beaten egg and stir to combine. The mixture should be thick and sticky enough to hold its shape when formed into a ball.

Using your fingers, roll the filling into golf ball–size rounds. (If the balls do not hold together well, you can add another ½ cup bread crumbs, or chill the filling for 30 minutes.) Place the finished boulettes on a baking sheet and refrigerate for at least 30 minutes.

Heat 2½ to 3 inches of oil in a large pot or cast-iron skillet to 350°F.

Roll each ball in flour, dip in buttermilk, and then roll through the remaining bread crumbs.

Working in batches so as not to overcrowd the pot, fry the boulettes (they should be submerged in oil) until golden and crusty, about 3 minutes, then drain on a plate lined with paper towels.

NOTE: If you don't have buttermilk in your fridge, you can use an equal amount of milk combined with one beaten egg.

# Boudin-stuffed Beignets (*Oreilles de Cochon*)

MAKES 9 BEIGNETS

*Oreilles de cochon* literally means "pig ears." But fear not: The name refers only to the way these boudin-stuffed beignets look after they've been fried. This is my version of another of my favorite dishes from Café des Amis, and a favorite hearty breakfast at the lake.

The rich, slightly spicy boudin mixture makes the perfect stuffing for the warm, crisp beignets, with a dusting of confectioners' sugar. The dough from Aunt Linda's homemade rolls forms the addictively tender beignet and is simple to prepare. You'll need only half that recipe here, but make it all and you can freeze the remaining dough for another time, or double the filling and freeze half of the uncooked beignets. (You could also simply shape the remaining dough into rolls and bake them for dinner.)

½ recipe Linda Zaunbrecher's Homemade Rolls (page 168)
1 cup My Boudin filling, removed from casings (page 30)

Vegetable oil, for frying
About 1 cup confectioners' sugar, for dusting

Dust a clean work surface with flour and roll the dough into a 14-inch square. Cut the dough into nine equal pieces.

Working with one piece at a time, place the square in front of you, with a corner pointing toward you. Place a generous tablespoon of boudin mixture across the diamond, leaving a ½-inch border on each side. Roll the bottom up over the boudin and fold in the corners and roll over one more time. There should be a triangular flap of dough left at the top, hence the ear shape. Repeat with the remaining dough and boudin. At this point the beignets can be fried right away, chilled on a baking sheet for several hours, or frozen.

Heat 2 to 3 inches of oil in a large, deep skillet to 350°F. Add the beignets, working in batches to avoid overcrowding, and fry for 3 to 4 minutes. You will need to hold the beignets down gently in the oil as they fry to ensure even cooking, or you can flip each one over halfway through cooking. Transfer the beignets to a plate lined with paper towels. Serve the beignets warm, dusted with confectioners' sugar.

# Chicken and Bacon Hash

SERVES 3 TO 4

One night, when my family and I were at our fish camp at Toledo Bend, I prepared too much barbecued chicken, as I often do. The leftovers inspired this hash for breakfast the next morning. You can also make this recipe with store-bought chicken (barbecued or even roasted). I am a huge fan of hearty breakfasts, and this flavorful hash fits the bill—especially when it's topped with eggs (over easy or soft-scrambled with Parmesan) and several dashes of hot sauce. If you're feeling decadent, this dish is also outstanding with poached eggs and hollandaise sauce.

Think of this recipe merely as a guide for ingredients that you happen to have on hand. For instance, I have also made this recipe with other leftover meats such as duck, braised pork, and pot roast.

1 medium russet potato, peeled
Salt
1 tablespoon olive oil
2 strips thick-sliced bacon, cut into
    ½-inch cubes
1 small onion, finely chopped
1 celery stalk, finely chopped
1 garlic clove, minced
1 jalapeño pepper, stemmed, seeded, and
    finely chopped
1½ teaspoons chopped fresh sage or thyme
½ teaspoon paprika

¼ teaspoon cayenne pepper
Ground black pepper
2½ to 3 cups shredded cooked chicken,
    preferably from leftover BBQ chicken
    (see Note)
2 tablespoons to ¼ cup chicken broth or
    water
½ bunch scallions (white and green
    parts), thinly sliced
1 tablespoon vegetable oil or rendered
    bacon fat
Flour for dusting

Cut the potato into a small dice and place in a small saucepan. Cover with 2 inches of water and add a generous pinch of salt. Bring the potato to a boil, reduce the heat to low, and simmer until tender, 13 to 15 minutes. Drain the potato and set aside.

Heat the olive oil in a large skillet over medium-high heat. Add the bacon and sauté until the fat renders and bacon is lightly browned but still soft, 3 to 4 minutes. Add the onion, celery, garlic, jalapeño, sage, paprika, cayenne, and black pepper, and a sprinkling of salt and cook, stirring, until softened and fragrant, 4 to 6 minutes.

Add the chicken and broth and cook over medium-high heat, stirring frequently to break up the meat, 6 to 8 minutes. Add the potato and continue to cook, stirring well to break up the pieces (they will help bind the mixture), until the liquid has completely been absorbed, 4 to 6 minutes. Taste for seasonings, adding more salt and pepper as desired, and stir in the scallions and allow the mixture to cool (for fastest results, spread the hash on a baking sheet and refrigerate).

Form the hash into 3- to 4-inch patties. Heat the oil or bacon fat in a large cast-iron skillet over medium-high heat. Sprinkle the hash patties on both sides with flour, then add them and fry until golden brown and crisp, 3 to 4 minutes on each side.

NOTE: The crisp patties will have the best texture if you shred the chicken very finely.

# Grilled Oysters with Garlic-Chile Butter

SERVES 4 TO 6

When I decided to buy a wood-burning oven for Cochon, this was one of the dishes I had in mind for it. The oven was installed a few weeks before the restaurant was ready to open, and this was the first dish we cooked at the restaurant two weeks before opening. We got a case of wine from Herbsaint and popped the oysters and baked them for our close friends and family. The spicy garlicky butter is a great match for the oysters baking in their shells. The anchovy (which you won't even know is in there) and the lemon really bring out the natural briny flavor of the oysters.

This recipe relies on a grill, but I've also had great results cooking these straight on the coals of a BBQ or campfire.

Compound butter
1 cup (2 sticks) butter
3 garlic cloves
2 anchovy fillets
Zest and juice of 1 lemon
2 tablespoons Vietnamese garlic chili
  sauce (see Note, page 60)

2 teaspoons red pepper flakes
¼ teaspoon cayenne pepper
1 teaspoon salt

16 oysters, in the shell
Lemon wedges, for garnish

Cut the butter into 1-inch cubes and allow it to soften to room temperature.

Mince the garlic, anchovy, and lemon zest (or mash in a mortar and pestle), and then fold in the butter, lemon juice, garlic chili sauce, red pepper flakes, cayenne, and salt. Roll the butter into a log, wrap in plastic, and refrigerate until needed.

Open the oysters as you would for on the half shell, discarding the top shells. Place a 1-tablespoon slice of the compound butter on each oyster and place on a hot grill until the juices begin to bubble and the oyster curls up around the edges, 6 to 10 minutes. (It's good to melt a few tablespoons of the butter to put on the oysters after they are grilled, in case some spills out of the shells.)

Serve immediately, with wedges of fresh lemon, if desired.

# Catfish Fried in Bacon Fat

SERVES 4

I don't know if it is a Southern thing, or a holdover from another era, but when I was a kid it seemed that everyone had a coffee can full of bacon grease under the sink. The first time I saw one I was confused—it's not a pretty sight—but saving bacon fat makes perfect sense to me now. People tend to be wary of cooking with bacon fat (whenever I save it at home it tends to disappear; I think my wife feels it's bad for me), but to me it's one of the best things in the world. If you're cooking bacon anyway, it's free and it makes other foods taste delicious.

Grandad Adams prepared catfish this way all the time at the lake, using the fresh fish he caught on his catfish lines. With a ready supply of white cornmeal and bacon grease (from the coffee can under the sink), it was a cheap and satisfying meal. It's easy to find farmed catfish in most stores, but if you can get your hands on freshly caught river or lake fish, they are definitely better. Some people have an aversion to catfish, or even think it tastes like dirt. I never understood that one. I think that we have become so accustomed to bland, tasteless farm-raised fish that we avoid fish with character.

This preparation works best in a cast-iron skillet. If you don't have one, I suggest that you go out immediately and buy one. Mine is a cherished possession—and the one and only piece of kitchen equipment I dug out of my flooded house after Katrina.

The spice level that I've suggested is a good starting point. I like my catfish extra spicy, so I would add even more cayenne and black pepper. My favorite condiment here is a really spicy cocktail sauce with lots of lemon and horseradish, but tartar sauce is also a good choice. In the best of all possible worlds, you'll have a bit of both on your plate.

| | |
|---|---|
| 1 cup white cornmeal | ¼ teaspoon cayenne pepper |
| ⅓ cup all-purpose flour | ⅛ teaspoon ground white pepper |
| 1 tablespoon salt | 2 (12-ounce) catfish fillets, sliced into |
| ¼ teaspoon ground black pepper, or more | 2-inch chunks |
| to taste | 6 tablespoons rendered bacon fat |

Whisk together the cornmeal and flour in a large bowl. In a small bowl, whisk together the salt, black pepper, cayenne, and white pepper. Sprinkle the catfish with the seasonings and allow the fish to "marinate" for at least 10 minutes at room temperature, or cover with plastic and refrigerate even longer (up to 1 day is fine). This step will make the fish "sweat," giving it some moisture for the flour to cling to.

When you're ready to cook, toss the catfish pieces with the cornmeal mixture. Transfer the catfish pieces to a plate or baking sheet, dusting off excess flour.

Heat the bacon fat in a medium skillet over medium-high heat. Sprinkle a bit of cornmeal in the fat to test the heat: It will be hot enough when there is an instant foam and a nice sizzle. Add half of the fillets, dropping the fish away from you so you don't splatter yourself, and cook until evenly golden brown, 2 to 3 minutes on each side. Remove the first batch with a slotted spatula, drain them on paper towels, and immediately add the second batch and repeat. I like to give the fillets an extra grinding of black pepper when they come out of the fat.

Serve the fried fish immediately, with your favorite coleslaw and spicy cocktail sauce.

# Pan-Fried Bass with Lemon and Browned Butter

SERVES 4

In Louisiana, it's not uncommon for a neighbor to arrive at your door with a bag of fresh fish fillets, so it's essential to know a quick and easy cooking method that doesn't call for a lot of fussy ingredients. Delicate fillets of white fish don't need much seasoning—it's best to enjoy the clean, natural flavor of the fish. That's why I love this surprisingly sophisticated recipe, which relies mostly on two things I always have on hand: butter and fresh lemons.

This recipe is also great for trout and bone-in bluegills. (For bone-in fish substitute cornmeal for half of the flour, and allow a little more cooking time on each side of the fillet.)

| | |
|---|---|
| 4 (6-ounce) bass fillets | 6 tablespoons butter |
| Salt, ground black pepper, and cayenne pepper to taste | Juice of 1 lemon |
| | 1 teaspoon capers (optional) |
| 3 tablespoons all-purpose flour | 2 tablespoons chopped fresh parsley |
| 3 tablespoons olive oil | |

Lightly season the fillets with salt, pepper, and cayenne and sprinkle on both sides with flour. Heat the olive oil in a large cast-iron skillet over high heat. Sear the fish for 2 to 3 minutes, until lightly golden brown on each side. Transfer the fish to a serving plate.

Use paper towels to carefully wipe out any residual grease from the skillet, and return skillet to the heat. The skillet will already be hot, but let it get a little hotter, then add the butter and let it sizzle and turn brown (this will take about 30 seconds). When the butter turns a nutty brown, add the lemon juice, capers, and parsley. Swirl the skillet to combine the ingredients and remove from the heat. Serve the fish on warmed plates, with equal portions of the browned butter spooned over the top.

NOTE: Be sure to use a large sauté pan for cooking the fillets. When cooking delicate white fish, it's very important that they have plenty of room in the pan and that you cook them over high heat. I use a 12-inch stainless steel skillet, and I cook only two or three fillets at a time. Trout in particular cooks very quickly; once it's overcooked, as with any white fish, it will start to fall apart. Take the fish out when you think it is about 75 percent done and it will continue to cook with the residual heat and be perfectly moist.

# Camp BBQ Chicken

SERVES 6 TO 8

During our Katrina exile, I cooked a lot as a way of focusing my emotions and calming myself. We spent much of our time outdoors with my dad, especially at the lake, on the deck or on the boat. Time outdoors + cooking = grilling, so we grilled often.

I always feel somewhat unsatisfied when I go through the trouble of firing up a charcoal grill and, after waiting for the coals to be just right, spend a mere 5 minutes grilling a hamburger or steak. After that, it's all over—the perfectly glowing coals taunting me to cook something else. That's why I love cooking grilled chicken on the bone afterward.

Grilling chicken over charcoal or a wood fire can be a little tricky because of the flare-ups that can occur, but once you get it down it is really pretty easy. To keep things easy this recipe calls for using a gas grill, but I prefer to cook over coals because it tastes better.

We serve this savory chicken with black-eyed peas, potato salad, and grilled corn. I'm typically pretty indecisive about whether or not to use BBQ sauce or just plain olive oil. I like it without sauce because I can really taste the chicken and the smoke from the fire, but I really do like a good BBQ sauce, too, especially when potato salad is on the table. Ah, life's dilemmas . . .

1 (3- to 4-pound) chicken, cut into
   10 serving pieces (see Note, page 120)
Salt and pepper
Extra-virgin olive oil
6 to 10 fresh thyme sprigs

Seedless red pepper flakes (see Note,
   page 25) or cayenne, for garnish
Lemon wedges, for garnish
BBQ sauce (optional)

Place the chicken pieces on a baking sheet and season generously with salt and pepper. Drizzle the chicken with enough olive oil to coat lightly, and massage the oil and the fresh thyme sprigs into the chicken (gently crushing the leaves and stems into the chicken). Allow the chicken to marinate for 30 minutes at room temperature or up to 8 hours in the fridge. (Bring the meat to room temperature before cooking.)

Heat the grill to medium-high and lightly oil the grill. Put the thighs, wings, and legs on first. Place them over the coals on the edge, not directly over the center. As the chicken heats, the fat from the skin begins to render—if the chicken is right over the hottest spot on the grill, it will flare up. But by placing the chicken pieces around the perimeter you will render the fat, you will hear it dripping, and then it will slow down (see Note). After the chicken takes a nice color, about 20 minutes, lower the heat to medium, turn the pieces over, and move them more to the center of the grill. Place the breast pieces on the outside and cook them in the same manner, about 15 minutes more. The chicken will cook in 35 to 40 minutes total, or until the juices run clear when pierced with a knife. Do as much of the cooking as possible on the skin side of the meat so as not to dry out the flesh.

Serve with a fresh sprinkling of red pepper flakes, a squeeze of lemon juice, and some good olive oil, and BBQ sauce if desired.

NOTE: It's always a good idea to have a sprayer of water to control flames. Stick close to your fire so that if one piece blazes up, you can move it away quickly and spray the flame.

## COOKING WITH CHARCOAL

If you're lighting a fire, start with 2½ to 3 pounds of charcoal for one chicken. Let the coals flame and burn until they are evenly colored (the coals should be mostly white), then spread them in an even layer three to four coals thick. Place the grate on the grill and let it get super-hot. Test your grill by holding your hand 6 inches over the fire. If you can hold it there for no more than 5 to 10 seconds, then the grill is way too hot; if you can leave it there forever, then it is not hot enough—the heat needs to be somewhere in between.

Right before you put the chicken on the grill, use a lightly oiled rag to wipe the grill grates. Wipe any excess oil off the chicken pieces before placing them on the grill.

# Sausage Burgers with Roasted Chiles and Creole Mustard

SERVES 6

This sausage burger is a nice change of pace; there is nothing like the juicy, salty, smoky taste of grilled pork.

This dish partners roasted chiles and Italian cheese with Cajun ingredients like pork and mustard greens. We have mustard greens here that will make you cry—really, they're that spicy. Tender baby greens are less bitter and can be eaten raw; their peppery flavor is a nice contrast to the rich pork and sweet tomatoes. Arm yourself with a cold beer and plenty of napkins before you tackle this monster of a burger—it's got big flavors, and it's probably going to be messy.

2½ pounds ground pork shoulder
2 garlic cloves, finely chopped
1 tablespoon salt
1 teaspoon ground white pepper
1 teaspoon ground black pepper
1 teaspoon red pepper flakes
½ teaspoon cayenne pepper
¼ cup balsamic vinegar
1 teaspoon dried oregano (see Sidebar, page 210)
1 teaspoon dried thyme

To assemble
6 slices Fontina or Piave cheese
2 loaves ciabatta bread
Roasted Chiles (recipe follows)
Reserved oil from Roasted Chiles
Creole (or whole-grain) mustard
½ pound baby red mustard greens (or arugula)
2 to 3 Creole or beefsteak tomatoes

Gently combine the ground pork and seasonings in a large mixing bowl; do not overwork the meat or the burgers will be tough. Form into six patties.

Grill the patties over a hot grill for 4 to 5 minutes per side, until cooked through and no longer pink at the center. Top each burger with a slice of cheese just before it's finished cooking, so the cheese will begin to melt.

Cut the ciabatta into squares that will fit the sausage patties, and drizzle the cut sides with some of the reserved chile oil. Grill until golden and crisp, about 4 minutes.

Spread some Creole mustard on the bottom half of the grilled bread, top with a sausage patty, a spoonful of the Roasted Chiles, a handful of greens, and a tomato slice. Top with the second half of grilled bread and press down gently.

# Roasted Chiles

6 to 8 Hungarian or Anaheim chiles
1 sprig of fresh rosemary
4 garlic cloves, thinly sliced
½ cup extra-virgin olive oil

Heat a grill to a medium-high setting (if you are using charcoal, the coals should be mostly white). Roast the chiles on the grill, using tongs to turn until evenly charred, about 6 to 8 minutes. Place the chiles in a plastic bag to steam them for about 5 minutes. Using your fingers and a paring knife, stem, seed, and peel the chiles, then slice them in half.

Place the chile strips in a small saucepan with the rosemary, garlic, and olive oil. Simmer over medium-low heat for 10 minutes, then remove from heat. Strain the oil into a glass bowl and reserve the chiles (discard the rosemary).

## FRESH AND DRIED OREGANO

I don't generally use a lot of dried herbs, but I actually prefer dried oregano over fresh if it has been freshly dried.

To dry oregano, cut the sprigs about 4 inches from the ground and secure the stems so that they hold together in 1-inch bundles (or smaller if you live somewhere really humid). Cut a string about 12 inches long and tie one end around the stems and hang upside down in a dry place, like a closet or the pantry. Be sure the herbs are not touching anything on any side so that they dry evenly. Once they are dried (from 1 to 4 weeks, depending on where you live), shake the leaves off by placing the bundle or half bundle between your two hands and rubbing them back and forth as if you were trying to start a fire with a stick. You'll still have to pick out some of the stems, but this is a really good start. Put the dried leaves in an airtight jar or sealable plastic bag so that they retain freshness. You'll be surprised how powerful dried oregano can be when it's not your typical store-bought stuff.

# Grilled Pork Ribs with Spicy Coonass BBQ Sauce

SERVES 8 TO 10

There are people out there who are fanatical about barbecue and about all the regional styles of smoking and sauces. I am not one of them, though I am familiar with most versions, and have definitely eaten plenty whenever I have had the chance.

Which is not to say I don't have an opinion about ribs. I really love braising ribs until they are falling off the bone, but I also like them grilled, retaining a little texture and chew. That's just what this recipe is all about. The finished ribs are tender but still firm, so you get to tear the meat off with your teeth, and they seem to retain more of their natural pork flavor. When you grill ribs, hang out around the grill while you're cooking and drink beer.

When I developed this sauce, my goal was to come up with a tangy flavor that had a natural smokiness from bacon (and not liquid smoke). Using two vinegars allows me to get sweetness from the apple cider, and kick from the red wine. (I use two vinegars in other dishes as well—some varieties have a deeper flavor, while others offer more acidity.)

2 (1½- to -2-pound) racks of pork ribs, cut into 4- to 5-bone sections
3 tablespoons salt

2 teaspoons ground black pepper
2 tablespoons brown sugar
Spicy Coonass BBQ Sauce (recipe follows)

At least 1 hour before cooking, place the ribs on a baking sheet and massage with the salt, pepper, and brown sugar. Heat a grill to medium-high (if you are using charcoal, the coals should be mostly white) and brown the ribs on each side. Reduce the heat to low and cook, covered, for 2 to 3 hours, turning the meat every 30 minutes or so, until the meat is very tender. Open the grill (or add more coals) as necessary to maintain an even heat. About 10 minutes before you take the meat off the grill, brush the ribs with a generous amount of BBQ sauce.

When the meat is cooked, cover with foil until ready to serve. Serve the meat with coleslaw, potato salad, and additional BBQ sauce.

# Spicy Coonass BBQ Sauce

MAKES ABOUT 3½ CUPS

Be sure to serve the ribs with additional sauce on the side. Leftovers can be kept in the refrigerator for up to 1 month.

4 thick slices of bacon, finely chopped
1 small onion, minced
3 garlic cloves, minced
2 jalapeño peppers, stemmed, seeded, and minced
1 teaspoon red pepper flakes
2 (14-ounce) bottles of ketchup
¼ cup Dijon mustard
¼ cup plus 1 tablespoon brown sugar
3 tablespoons honey
¼ cup red wine vinegar
2 tablespoons apple cider vinegar
2 teaspoons Worcestershire sauce
1 teaspoon each salt, black pepper, and cayenne pepper
Juice of 1 medium lemon

Heat the bacon in a medium saucepan over medium-high heat. Cook until about one-third of the fat is rendered, then add the remaining ingredients and simmer for 30 to 35 minutes, stirring occasionally, until slightly thickened.

# Grilled Rib-Eye

SERVES 6 TO 8

This is my take on prime rib. Generally speaking, prime rib is a top-grade cut of meat (Prime grade vs. Choice or Select), but unfortunately many people serve a rib roast that is not Prime and it's often disappointing. If I go to the trouble of making a roast, I always use Prime. The extent of fat marbling is what makes it tasty—mouthwatering in a primal sense.

Cooking a rib-eye roast on the bone is great, but because a boneless cut is easier to grill, I've included a recipe for that. For the best flavor, season the meat with lots of salt and pepper at least two hours before cooking so the seasonings really permeate the meat. Then it's important to sear the meat over high heat, finish cooking it more slowly over a lower heat, and finally let it rest before serving—good rules of thumb for cooking any roasts, really.

I love the rich beef flavor that this roast delivers, and it's a great alternative to grilling steaks. I have to admit, though, that I like it better cold the next day for lunch—with sea salt, mustard, spicy greens like watercress or arugula, and a glass of good red wine.

The first time I grilled this rib-eye at Toledo Bend, there were chanterelle mushrooms sprouting up all over the woods. Cassidy and I went foraging, and we sautéed the mushrooms and covered our slices of meat with them. If you can find any kind of wild mushrooms, I recommend them as a side dish.

1 (4-pound) boneless rib-eye roast
Salt and ground black pepper
6 sprigs fresh thyme

Coarse sea salt
Extra-virgin olive oil

At least 2 hours before cooking the meat, place it on a sheet pan and generously coat with salt, pepper, and the thyme sprigs (massaging the stems and leaves into the meat). Don't hold back with the salt—it forms a flavorful crust on the outside that really gives the meat character and dimension. For best results, roll the meat over the seasonings that collect on the bottom of the pan as well, so you coat it as much as possible. Let the meat sit at room temperature for up to 2 hours, or overnight in the fridge (loosely covered, so it doesn't pick up other flavors from the fridge but with enough air so that it stays dry).

Get the grill as hot as it will go, then knock the temperature back to about 400°F. Brush off the thyme sprigs and sear the meat until it's browned and crusty, 5 to 7 minutes for each side. Close the grill as necessary to preserve heat if too much heat is escaping and the meat is not browning nicely.

Reduce the temperature to low (about 275°F) and cook the meat for 1½ to 2 hours, flipping it every 30 minutes or so, until the internal temperature is 145°F for rare (or longer, as desired).

Transfer the meat to a platter and let rest for at least 30 minutes (the meat will continue to cook; see Note). Slice the meat into generous 1-inch-thick slices, and top with a sprinkling of salt and a drizzle of olive oil.

NOTE: Resting the roast is extremely important. It will even out the cooking and allow the natural juices to settle back into the meat. If you slice the meat when it's too hot, the juices will run out and you'll be left with dry, tough meat.

# KILLER COCKTAILS

You can't be outside grilling oysters or boiling shellfish without a cold drink in your hand. Here are a few drinks that perk up everything from weekend brunches to backyard barbecues, or simply a lazy afternoon on the front porch.

# Absinthe Cocktail

SERVES 1

Authentic absinthe is finally legal in the United States. For years it was banned because it was said that the traditional wormwood aging process gave it hallucinogenic qualities that made people go crazy. Personally I think that may have had more to do with its extremely high alcohol content and the amount that people drank. Often mistakenly labeled a liqueur (absinthe is bottled without any added sugar) the liquor has a natural green color (hence its nickname, "the green fairy") though it is also available in a clear variety. I've experimented with several varieties, and I confess it was the drunkest I have ever been (and that is saying something). Its effect is somehow different from regular booze with the same alcohol content, with a trippy quality; one drink is good, the second is better, and a third is simply a bad, bad idea.

The coolest thing about absinthe, though, is not its disarming effect—it's the ritual that surrounds its consumption. Cold water drips out of an absinthe fountain over a sugar cube, dripping into the absinthe to mellow the strong licorice flavor and cool the drink down.

| | |
|---|---|
| 1 unrefined sugar cube | 1½ ounces absinthe |

Fill an absinthe fountain with ice water and place the sugar cube on an absinthe spoon. Pour the absinthe into a rocks glass and set the spoon on top. Allow water from the fountain to drip slowly over the sugar cube. As the sugar cube dissolves, watch for what is called the "louche," which is when the absinthe and water mixture becomes totally cloudy. As the glass fills, the layer of absinthe on top will get thinner and thinner; when it disappears completely, the drink is ready to be served.

# Cathy's Bloody Mary

MAKES 1 GENEROUS DRINK

This is my mother-in-law's famous (at least in our family) rendition of the classic. I find too often that this drink is too bland for my taste, but this version has plenty of kick. (Cathy thinks Tabasco is essential.) Fiery drinks are a staple for weekend brunches and football mornings.

2 ounces (4 tablespoons) vodka
1 cup tomato juice
½ cup Clamato juice
1 teaspoon Worcestershire sauce
¾ teaspoon Tabasco or other hot sauce
⅛ teaspoon celery seeds

1 teaspoon grated horseradish
Pinch of celery salt
Ground black pepper to taste
Juice of 1 lemon wedge
Pickled okra, for garnish
Celery stalk, for garnish

Fill a 16-ounce glass with ice cubes and add all the ingredients except okra and celery and stir well. Garnish with pickled okra and celery stalk.

# Bourbon Cherry Lemonade

MAKES 1 STOUT DRINK

1½ ounces (3 tablespoons) Woodford
    Reserve or other bourbon
1 ounce (2 tablespoons) sweet cherry juice

Lemonade, as needed
Bourbon-soaked maraschino cherry, for
    garnish (optional)

Fill a Collins glass with crushed ice. Combine the bourbon, the cherry juice, and crushed ice in a shaker. Shake vigorously, then strain into the Collins glass. Top off the glass with fresh lemonade and garnish with a cherry.

# Satsuma Old-Fashioned

MAKES 1 STOUT DRINK

Sometime around late November we start getting amazing locally grown Satsumas at the restaurants. The supersweet juice of this citrus fruit is a natural for desserts and cocktails. Combining Satsumas with good-quality bourbon and a few dashes of Peychaud's and orange-flavored bitters makes for a cocktail so delicious that you're bound to want another (buy plenty of Satsumas).

1 small Satsuma or tangerine, sliced
¼-inch thick (ends discarded)
1 maraschino cherry
2 dashes of Fee Brothers Orange Bitters

2 dashes of Peychaud bitters
¾ ounce simple syrup (recipe follows)
1½ ounces Makers Mark bourbon

In an old-fashioned glass (a short highball) muddle the Satsuma slices and the maraschino cherry with the bitters. Fill the glass with cubed ice, the simple syrup, the bourbon, and stir until blended.

## Simple Syrup

Equal parts sugar and water create what is referred to as a "heavy" sugar syrup. It's the one we prefer for cocktails.

8 ounces granulated sugar
1 cup water

Heat the sugar and water in a small saucepan over medium-low heat, stirring occasionally, until the sugar melts. Allow the syrup to cool and then store in the refrigerator until needed.

LOUISIANA SWEET TOOTH

Louisiana is famous for decadence, and its desserts are certainly no exception. All my most cherished childhood dessert memories are linked to a particular relative—Aunt Anne's Chocolate Yummy, Mom's Lemon Meringue Pie, Granny's German Chocolate Cake, and Aunt Arlene's Peanut Butter Fudge. Although we didn't get sweets all the time, anytime there were family get-togethers we could count on an abundance of options, especially around the holidays.

Southerners adore very sweet desserts. A lot of the confections we enjoyed while growing up were made with copious amounts of Pet Evaporated Milk and sugar. As much as I still love Aunt Arlene's Peanut Butter Fudge, I'm almost shocked at the amount of sugar needed to make it.

On the less cloying side of the sweetness scale is fresh fruit. I fondly remember eating peaches off of Grandad's trees, picking fresh strawberries from the field, and pulling blackberries from the thorny vines on a hot summer day—the kind of fruit you just can't buy in a store. I am fondest of desserts that let the beauty of fresh fruit stand front and center. I guess you can say I'm somewhat old-fashioned; as far as I'm concerned, nothing says "home cooking" like a perfect homemade apple pie.

Chocolate lovers will find a range of options and sophistication levels here, from the aforementioned Chocolate Yummy—a layered pudding dessert that your kids will love—to Chocolate Bread Pudding with two kinds of chocolate and Bourbon Sauce, and a Super-Rich Chocolate Pecan Tart that flies off the menu at Herbsaint. And because I think there is perhaps nothing more satisfying than homemade ice cream, I include recipes for two favorite flavors: buttermilk, which is delicious melting alongside a slice of hot apple pie, and blueberry, with a bright berry flavor as dense as its deep purple color.

# Chocolate Yummy

SERVES 6 TO 8

Chocolate Yummy might not be part of your dessert vernacular, but in Cajun Country, everybody knows what this dish is. The "yummy" architecture begins with a base of crumbled cookies (usually store-bought), followed by layers of sweetened cream cheese, chocolate pudding, and Cool Whip. I have a few aunts who specialize in this dessert, so it never fails to conjure up memories of family get-togethers. This is the type of dessert that someone pulls out of the fridge after a big meal or cookout, and even when guests think they're too full, they find themselves polishing off a portion of yummy.

Here is a grown-up version that's a bit more sophisticated, because I have lost my taste for the super-sweet original. Here, a rich pecan shortbread base is topped with cream cheese, a silky pudding made with dark chocolate, and fresh whipped cream. I'm pretty sure it would even win my aunts' approval.

Pecan shortbread
3 ounces pecans, toasted
3 tablespoons granulated sugar
½ cup (1 stick) butter
½ teaspoon vanilla extract
1 cup all-purpose flour
½ teaspoon salt

Chocolate pudding
1 cup heavy cream
¼ cup granulated sugar
3 egg yolks

3½ ounces dark chocolate, coarsely chopped
1 ounce milk chocolate, coarsely chopped
1 tablespoon butter
¼ teaspoon vanilla extract
Pinch of salt

1 pound cream cheese
½ cup plus 2 tablespoons confectioners' sugar
2 cups heavy cream
Chocolate shavings, for garnish

Place the pecans and sugar in a food processor and pulse together for 30 seconds.

In the bowl of an electric mixer, cream together the butter, vanilla, and the pecan-sugar mixture, then stir in the flour and salt until just mixed. Chill the dough for 30 minutes.

Preheat the oven to 325°F.

Use your fingers to press the chilled dough into a 9-inch square baking dish. Prick the dough with a fork and bake 10 to 15 minutes, until lightly golden. Cool the cooked dough while preparing the remaining layers.

Heat the cream for the pudding in a heavy-bottomed saucepan over medium heat. Stir together the sugar and egg yolks in a mixing bowl. When the cream is hot (but not boiling), temper the cream into the yolks by slowly adding half the cream while stirring vigorously, then stir the egg mixture back into the cream in the saucepan. Cook over medium-low heat for 5 to 7 minutes, until it is thick enough to coat the back of a spoon.

Place the dark and milk chocolate in a mixing bowl with the butter, vanilla, and salt. Pour the hot cream mixture over the chocolate and stir until the chocolate and butter are melted. Spread the pudding in a shallow dish to cool and cover it with a piece of plastic wrap placed directly on the surface so a skin does not form.

In a small mixing bowl or the bowl of an electric mixer, beat the cream cheese and ½ cup confectioners' sugar together until smooth.

In the bowl of an electric mixer, or by hand, whip the cream to soft peaks, then add the remaining 2 tablespoons sugar and whip a few minutes more, until stiff peaks form.

Spread the cream cheese over the cooled shortbread crust, top with the pudding, and then add the whipped cream. Refrigerate for at least 1 hour, or overnight. Garnish with additional chocolate shavings, if desired.

# Peanut Butter Fudge

MAKES 16 SQUARES

We could count on finding a decorative tin of peanut butter fudge at my aunt Arlene's or my granny's house almost any time, especially at family get-togethers. When my sister and I would arrive, we'd immediately start snooping around for the creamy, tan-colored squares—as a kid, I could eat a lot of fudge. This recipe reflects the way I remember it, but you may want to cut the sugar a bit if you don't like overly sweet desserts. The fudge is great with super-strong coffee, a single-barrel bourbon, or on a dessert platter with an assortment of cookies and bars.

4 tablespoons (½ stick) butter
1 teaspoon vanilla extract
2 cups brown sugar, packed
½ cup heavy cream

1 cup creamy peanut butter
2 cups confectioners' sugar
½ cup peanuts, toasted and chopped

Heat the butter and vanilla in a medium saucepan over medium heat. When the butter melts, stir in the brown sugar and cream, bring to a boil, and cook, stirring, for 2 minutes. Stir in the peanut butter and mix until smooth. Remove from the heat and cool slightly.

Transfer the mixture to the bowl of an electric mixer fitted with the paddle attachment. Add the confectioners' sugar and beat at medium speed for 2 to 3 minutes, until smooth.

Line a square 8-inch baking dish with buttered parchment or waxed paper. Pour in the peanut butter mixture, top with the chopped peanuts, and let cool completely. To serve, cut the fudge into 2-inch squares.

# Chocolate Bread Pudding with Bourbon Sauce

SERVES 6 TO 8

Bread pudding is probably the most famous dessert in New Orleans, and in most places in the South, especially in restaurants. It's a fantastic—and economical—way to transform leftover bread. White French bread yields traditional flavor and texture, though I have also made good variations using ciabatta bread (and some people use brioche or even croissants). Dry, day-old bread delivers the best results, but if your bread is too soft you can always put it in the oven for a few minutes to crisp it (this will give the pudding a little more texture when it's cooked).

This recipe is decadent with white and dark chocolate and a rich, sticky bourbon sauce—it's the ultimate way to indulge in bread pudding. But feel free to add raisins, dried cranberries, or dried cherries. On a recent trip to France, I used fresh Bing cherries and white chocolate.

2 quarts dried bread cubes, in 1-inch pieces
4 ounces white chocolate, coarsely chopped
4 ounces dark chocolate, coarsely chopped
3 large eggs
1 quart half-and-half
¾ cup sugar
2 teaspoons ground cinnamon
1 tablespoon vanilla extract
¼ cup (½ stick) butter, melted
Bourbon Sauce (recipe follows)

Preheat the oven to 350°F.

Grease a 9 x 13-inch baking pan. Spread the bread in the baking pan. Sprinkle the white and dark chocolate over the bread.

Whisk the eggs, half-and-half, sugar, cinnamon, vanilla, and melted butter together in a large bowl and pour over the bread. The mixture should look fairly wet and the bread should be slightly submerged when pressed with a spatula.

Bake, uncovered, for about 30 minutes, until the bread pudding jiggles like a bowl of jelly. If only the middle jiggles, it needs more time—the pudding should hold together and jiggle as one piece. Allow the pudding to cool slightly, then serve with a generous drizzle of Bourbon Sauce.

# Bourbon Sauce

¼ cup sugar
½ cup (1 stick) butter
2 egg yolks
2 to 4 tablespoons bourbon

Heat the sugar and butter in a small saucepan over low heat, stirring, until the butter melts and the sugar dissolves. Place the egg yolks in a metal mixing bowl and slowly pour the warm butter into the bowl, whisking constantly. Finish the sauce with the bourbon, depending on how strong you want the flavor to be. If you are not serving the sauce immediately, cover and keep it warm. If the sauce gets too hot or too cold, it will break; if this happens, you'll need to whisk in another egg to fix it.

# Granny's German Chocolate Cake

MAKES ONE 10-INCH LAYER CAKE

As kids, my sister and I always hoped to find something sweet when we arrived at Granny's house, and we were rarely disappointed. Our usual discoveries were Rice Krispies treats, Popsicles, peanut butter fudge, pralines, and homemade cookies, but the real jackpot was walking in and seeing a German chocolate cake gleaming under a glass dome. You could count on this special cake to make an appearance on holidays and special occasions, but every once in a while it would be waiting for us for no reason at all.

Anne Weatherford, my first pastry chef at Herbsaint, gave me a recipe for a chocolate blackout cake, which is a rich and moist chocolate cake that I use as the base for this traditional recipe. I've had fillings for this cake that were either too dry or overly sweet, but this one is an irresistible balance of sweetness and creaminess. The result is an admittedly updated—but irresistible— rendition of Granny's classic.

| Coconut-pecan filling | Cake |
|---|---|
| 3 cups sugar | 2⅓ cups all-purpose flour |
| 1½ cups (3 sticks) butter | 1½ cups unsweetened cocoa powder |
| 3 cups evaporated milk | 1½ teaspoons salt |
| 12 egg yolks (beaten) | 1 tablespoon baking soda |
| 3 cups flaked sweetened coconut | 1 tablespoon baking powder |
| 3 cups chopped pecans | 3 cups sugar |
| 3 teaspoons vanilla extract | 5 large eggs |
| | 1½ cups well-shaken buttermilk |
| | 1½ cups strong coffee |
| | 12 tablespoons (1½ sticks) butter, melted |

Combine the sugar, butter, evaporated milk, and egg yolks for the filling in a saucepan. Cook over medium heat, stirring, until thickened, 10 to 15 minutes. Cool for about 20 minutes, then fold in the coconut, pecans, and vanilla. (See Note.)

Preheat the oven to 350°F. Butter and flour three 10-inch round cake pans.

Sift the flour, cocoa, salt, baking soda, baking powder, and sugar for the cake into a large bowl and whisk to combine.

In another bowl, whisk together the eggs, buttermilk, and coffee. Stir the egg mixture into the dry ingredients. Add the melted butter and stir to combine.

Divide the batter among the prepared pans and gently tap the pans on the counter to pop any air bubbles. Bake until springy and firm to the touch, and a cake

tester inserted into the center of the cake comes out mostly dry, about 25–30 minutes (for even baking, rotate the pans after 20 minutes).

Let the cakes cool in the pans for 10 minutes, then run a paring knife around the rim of the pans, invert the cakes onto on a cooling rack, and cool completely.

Level the cake tops with a long slicing or serrated knife, slicing off the rounded portions on top (discard or eat as a snack). Using a plastic spatula, spread the coconut mixture on the bottom cake, then place the second cake layer on top. Frost the top of the second layer, then place the third layer on top of it, then cover the top and sides with the coconut filling. To serve, cut the cake with a long slicer knife, wiping it off with a warm, wet towel in between slices.

NOTE: The coconut filling tends to thicken on standing, so don't be tempted to add more coconut up front.

# Fresh Peach Buckle

SERVES 6

Unlike cobber, which is fruit topped with a sweetened biscuit-like batter, buckle has the batter folded right into the juicy fruit. The result is a rustic cakelike dessert that is all about the flavor of fresh fruit. I make this recipe all summer long, when the peaches at the farmers' market are at their sweetest. This recipe gets added flavor from an easy-to-make spicy crumble topping. Topped with a scoop of homemade vanilla ice cream, this is the perfect summertime dessert; however, it also makes a delicious breakfast the next day, with a cup of super-strong coffee with cream.

Buckle batter
1 cup milk
4 eggs
2 teaspoons vanilla extract
3½ cups all-purpose flour
1 tablespoon baking powder
1 teaspoon salt
1 cup (2 sticks) butter, at room
    temperature
1 cup granulated sugar
5 medium peaches, peeled, seeded, and
    cut into 1-inch cubes (about 3 cups)

Crumble topping
1 cup all-purpose flour
4 tablespoons (½ stick) butter, cut into
    pieces
¼ cup granulated sugar
¼ cup brown sugar
½ teaspoon ground cinnamon

Preheat the oven to 350°F. Butter a 9 x 13-inch baking dish.

In a small bowl, combine the milk, eggs, and vanilla. In a separate bowl, whisk together the flour, baking powder, and salt.

In the bowl of an electric mixer fitted with the paddle attachment, cream the butter and sugar on medium speed until light and fluffy, about 2 minutes. Reduce the speed to low and alternately add the dry and wet ingredients (beginning and ending with the dry), until the batter is smooth. Add the peaches and stir by hand until just combined.

Scrape the batter into the prepared baking dish. In a small bowl, use a fork or your fingers to combine the crumble topping ingredients. Crumble the topping over the batter and bake for about 45 minutes, until the buckle is golden on top and springy to the touch. Serve warm or at room temperature.

# Caramelized Apple Upside-Down Cake

SERVES 6 TO 8

*Tarte tatin,* the classic French dessert of caramelized apples atop a flaky pastry, is a weakness of mine—but so is good old pineapple upside-down cake. So you can understand why I love this cake, which is somewhere between the two.

This cake is a delicious way to experience the wonders of caramelized apples with a moist, down-home cake that soaks up all the sweet juices. I think Granny Smith apples offer the best flavor, but you can use other firm and tart varieties as well. The addition of star anise and cardamom add an exotic perfume.

At Herbsaint we serve this with cinnamon ice cream, but you can't go wrong with a scoop of vanilla, preferably homemade.

6 tablespoons (¾ stick) butter, at room temperature
¾ cup sugar plus 2 teaspoons
1¾ cups all-purpose flour
½ tablespoon baking powder
½ teaspoon salt
¾ teaspoon ground cinnamon
3 large eggs
1 teaspoon vanilla extract
¼ teaspoon ground ginger
⅔ cup sour cream

For apples
6 Granny Smith apples
2 cups sugar
½ cup water
6 tablespoons cold butter, cut into small pieces
½ tablespoon ground cardamom
1 tablespoon ground star anise

Preheat the oven to 325°F. Generously grease a 10-inch cake pan with 1 tablespoon of the butter and then dust with 2 teaspoons of the sugar, shaking out excess.

Whisk together the flour, baking powder, salt, and cinnamon.

In the bowl of an electric mixer fitted with the paddle attachment, beat the remaining 5 tablespoons butter and ¾ cup sugar on medium speed until light and creamy, about 2 minutes. Add the eggs, one at a time, beating until incorporated, and then add the vanilla, ginger, and sour cream; mix until just combined. Stir in the dry ingredients slowly, until just combined, then refrigerate the batter for 2 hours.

Peel and core the apples and cut into 1½-inch chunks.

Heat the sugar and water in a large, deep sauté pan over medium heat and cook the sugar-water mixture until it caramelizes to a medium brown color, 12 to 14 minutes. (You can gently shake the pan and occasionally brush down the sides

of the pan with water, but try not to stir the mixture or the sugar will stick to the spoon and the sides of the pan.) Whisk in the butter.

Combine the apples, cardamom, and star anise in a medium bowl and toss to combine. Add the apples to the caramel and cook over medium-high heat for about 5 minutes, until the apples are dark golden and caramelized, but still firm; remove from heat and set aside.

Evenly spread the apples with all the caramel in the bottom of the prepared cake pan. Spread the batter over the apples, making sure to go all the way to the edges of the dish. Bake until the top of the cake is golden brown and springy to the touch, about 30 minutes. Allow the cake to rest in the baking pan for 30 minutes.

Run a paring knife around the rim of the cake, place a serving plate on top of the pan, and invert the cake onto the plate. Use a spatula to scrape any remaining apples and caramel onto the cake. Serve warm or at room temperature.

# Super-Rich Chocolate Pecan Tart

MAKES ONE 10-INCH TART

This tart is a close relative of pecan pie, with a dose of chocolate. When I was trying to quit smoking, I would slice it into thin pieces and eat it like a candy bar. (I'm one of those people who get a buzz from chocolate, so it's satisfying and relaxes my nerves.) At Herbsaint we serve this tart at room temperature, but I actually prefer it cold.

*Pasta frolla,* an Italian pie dough, works best for this tart because it holds up to the heavier filling and doesn't crumble when sliced. I also find that this dough is a little more forgiving. If the dough is tearing a lot, you can add a little more flour and knead it a little, and it should work better.

1 cup sugar
½ cup water
1¼ cups heavy cream
2 eggs
1 egg yolk
1 tablespoon butter
1 teaspoon vanilla extract
1 cup pecan pieces, toasted

1 Pasta Frolla Crust
  (recipe follows), prebaked

Chocolate glaze
6 ounces semisweet chocolate, coarsely
  chopped
¾ cup heavy cream
2 tablespoons corn syrup
1 teaspoon vanilla extract

Heat the sugar and water in a medium saucepan over medium heat until the mixture caramelizes (it will be the color of a caramel candy). Watch the pan closely; once it starts to caramelize it will go quickly.

In a separate pan, bring the cream just to a boil. Stir the hot cream into the caramelized sugar and cook 3 more minutes, until the mixture forms a smooth caramel. Remove from the heat and cool for 15 to 20 minutes.

Preheat the oven to 350°F.

Stir the eggs, yolk, butter, and vanilla into the caramel. Be sure the mixture is not too hot or it will scramble the eggs and you will have to start over.

Scatter the pecan pieces into the pie crust and pour the sugar mixture over the top. Bake the tarts for 20 to 30 minutes, or until set. Cool the tart completely on a wire rack.

Place the chocolate in a mixing bowl. Heat the cream and corn syrup to a boil and pour over the chocolate. Add the vanilla and stir slowly once the chocolate begins to melt. The chocolate glaze should be smooth and pourable.

Top the tart with the chocolate glaze and refrigerate to set the chocolate.

# Pasta Frolla Crust

When rolling this dough, use ample flour on your board and on top of the dough. I do an initial roll to about ½ to 1 inch thick, dust the top with flour, and flip it over, then dust again, but you may require less (it's so hot here that dough gets soft pretty quick).

14 tablespoons (1¾ sticks) butter
½ cup sugar
Pinch of salt
2 egg yolks
½ teaspoon vanilla extract
2⅓ to 3 cups all-purpose flour

Preheat the oven to 350°F.

In the bowl of an electric mixer fitted with a paddle attachment, beat the butter, sugar, and salt together until light and fluffy. Add the yolks and vanilla, and mix, then stir in the flour until just combined. Transfer the mixture to a counter and knead until it comes together and feels supple and smooth.

Roll the dough out on a well-floured work surface until it is ¼ inch thick. To place the dough round in a tart pan, roll it around a well-floured rolling pin and unroll it over the tart pan, gently pressing it into the pan. Trim off excess.

If it tears you can use other pieces to patch the dough together in the pan.

With the tines of a fork, prick the bottom of the crust so it doesn't puff up during baking. Chill the crust for 1 hour, then bake for 10 minutes and cool completely before filling.

# Strawberries with Cornmeal Shortcakes and Fresh Whipped Cream

SERVES 8

One of my earliest food memories is my first strawberry. It was a hot and dry day in Louisiana, and we were driving north of Lake Charles for the sole purpose of picking strawberries. When we got to the farm, we each got a straw basket and walked out into the field to pick our bounty. The first one I found was dark red and super-sweet, and the juice exploded when I bit into it. On a recent trip to Burgundy with my family, I was reminded of that day. We stayed at a farmhouse and the strawberries in the rough garden out back were the only I've had since that came close to that amazing flavor.

I have been accused sometimes of not liking fruit. That couldn't be further from the truth; what I don't like is underripe, hard fruit that's out of season. These days, strawberries are often picked too early for shipping, so I save this recipe for that special crop of perfect strawberries at the peak of the season, even if that's only once or twice a year.

The point of covering the strawberries in sugar is not only to sweeten them up but also to create the juice that will soak into the bottom layer of the shortcake. If the strawberries are super-sweet, use less sugar.

1 quart ripe strawberries, hulled and rinsed
¼ to ½ cup granulated sugar

Shortcakes
1 cup all-purpose flour
1 cup fine cornmeal
½ cup granulated sugar
2 teaspoons baking powder
¼ cup lard, cold

2 tablespoons butter, cold
Pinch of salt
1 egg
½ cup milk

Whipped cream
2 cups heavy cream
2 tablespoons confectioners' sugar
½ teaspoon vanilla extract

Cut the strawberries into quarters and toss with the sugar. Let sit for a few hours to give the sugar time to extract some juice.

Preheat the oven to 400°F. Place a rack in the highest position.

Combine the flour, sugar, cornmeal, and baking powder in a mixing bowl. Add the lard, butter, and salt and cut into the flour with a pastry cutter or your fingertips.

Whisk the eggs and milk together and stir into the dry ingredients.

Drop the batter onto a lightly buttered sheet pan with a tablespoon and form into biscuits about 3 inches in diameter. Bake for 15 minutes on the top rack, until lightly golden. (If you have a convection oven, now would be a good time to use it.) Cool on a rack.

Pour the cream into a large mixing bowl or the bowl of an electric mixer and whip until soft peaks form. Add the confectioners' sugar and vanilla, and beat a few minutes more, until soft peaks form.

Cut the biscuits in half and place a heaping spoon of strawberries with juice on top. Cover with whipped cream, replace the biscuit top, and add another dollop of whipped cream.

# Satsuma Buttermilk Pie

MAKES ONE 9- OR 10-INCH PIE

This creamy, refreshing dessert gets a sunny flavor from satsumas—juicy, tangerine-like oranges that flourish in the South. The seeming richness of buttermilk makes this the perfect accompaniment to fresh berries, especially blackberries and blueberries. I've included a recipe for a homemade graham cracker crust, but in a pinch the store-bought will work just fine. You can also substitute fresh lemon juice and zest for the satsumas, but you'll want to add an extra ¼ cup sugar.

½ cup plus 2 tablespoons sugar
3 tablespoons all-purpose flour
4 large eggs
4 tablespoons (½ stick) butter, melted
1 cup buttermilk, well shaken
1 teaspoon vanilla extract

1 teaspoon finely grated satsuma
   orange or tangerine or lemon zest
3 tablespoons satsuma orange or
   tangerine or lemon juice
1 10-inch Graham Cracker Pie Crust
   (recipe follows), prebaked

Preheat the oven to 300°F.

Whisk together the sugar and flour, then add the eggs, one at a time, until well combined. Slowly whisk in the melted butter. Whisk in the buttermilk, vanilla, and zest and juice, and pour into the pie shell. Bake for 30 minutes, or until the mixture is just set. Serve this pie at room temperature, or chilled, with whipped cream and fresh berries, if desired.

## Graham Cracker Pie Crust

½ cup (1 stick) butter
2 tablespoons light brown sugar
4 tablespoons granulated sugar
2 tablespoons honey

¾ cup all-purpose flour
¼ cup whole wheat flour
½ teaspoon salt
¼ teaspoon ground cinnamon

In a large mixing bowl or the bowl of an electric mixer, cream the butter and sugars. Add the honey, flours, salt, and cinnamon, and stir until just combined. Refrigerate the dough for at least 2 hours or up to 1 day in advance.

Preheat the oven to 325°F.

Use your hands to press the dough into a 9- or 10-inch pie pan. Bake about 30 minutes, or until lightly browned. Cool completely before filling.

# Blueberry Cobbler

SERVES 6 TO 8

Cobblers can be made with almost any fruit, of course, but as far as I'm concerned they are never better than when the biscuit-like top crowns a bubbling pool of dark purple berries. Then again, I'm something of a berry freak. The only thing I don't like about blueberries is their short season. At my restaurants, we serve blueberries only during the summer, when they are local—ripened by the warm southern sun and bursting with flavor. I'm equally fond of Louisiana blackberries and they work equally well in this recipe.

Biscuit dough
1½ cups all-purpose flour
⅓ cup granulated sugar
3 teaspoons baking powder
Pinch of salt
½ teaspoon ground cinnamon
½ cup (1 stick) butter
1 large egg, beaten
½ cup milk

¾ cup sugar
2 tablespoons cornstarch
⅓ cup water
6 cups blueberries
Zest and juice of ½ lemon
½ teaspoon vanilla extract

Crumble topping
⅓ cup brown sugar, packed
⅓ cup butter
¾ cup all-purpose flour

Preheat the oven to 400°F.

Combine the flour, ⅓ cup sugar, baking powder, salt, and cinnamon in a bowl (or food processor) and cut in the butter until the mixture is coarse and crumbly.

In a separate bowl, whisk the egg and milk together and then stir into the dry ingredients to form the cake batter; set aside.

Combine the sugar and cornstarch with the water in a saucepan. Heat until the sugar dissolves, then add the blueberries, lemon zest and juice, and vanilla and simmer over medium heat for about 5 minutes.

Pour the blueberry mixture into a buttered 8 x 12-inch baking dish. Top the fruit with spoonfuls of the batter (the batter does not need to cover the berries completely; it will expand during baking).

Mix the brown sugar, butter, and flour, then sprinkle over the dollops of batter. Bake for 25 to 30 minutes, until the top is lightly browned and the dough has cooked through. Straight-from-the-oven cobblers are molten—allow this to cool for at least 20 minutes before serving.

# Apple Pie with Buttermilk Ice Cream

MAKES ONE 10-INCH PIE

One of the best things about baking apple pie is the aroma of it as it bakes, permeating the house.

We've all heard the expression "American as apple pie," yet pies made with the same ingredients can be so different from one another. When we tested this recipe, we all agreed it was the best apple pie we'd ever had.

How you work the dough is critical to the success of this pie. Make sure to be light-fingered and try to leave some chunks of butter and lard speckled through the dough. It's also critical to let the pie cool before slicing it; as tempting as it is to dig in, a cool pie will yield better-looking slices. Creamy buttermilk ice cream has a slight tartness that pairs well with the spicy juices of the apples; however, a premium store-bought vanilla ice cream will do just fine.

5 Granny Smith apples
½ cup (1 stick) butter
1 cup sugar, plus extra for top
Juice of ½ lemon
¼ teaspoon vanilla extract
1 teaspoon ground cinnamon

¼ teaspoon grated nutmeg
1 large egg, lightly beaten
Sugar, for garnish
Dough for Flaky Pie Crust (page 247),
    chilled but not prebaked
Buttermilk Ice Cream (recipe follows)

Preheat the oven to 350°F.

Peel, core, and thinly slice the apples into a large mixing bowl. Heat the butter, 1 cup sugar, and lemon juice together in a saucepan over medium heat until the butter and sugar melt, then pour over the apples. Add the vanilla, cinnamon, and nutmeg and toss to combine.

Divide the dough into two balls and roll out each half. Line the pie pan with the dough round and gently press it into the pan, leaving some excess hanging over the rim. Use a paring knife to trim evenly around the outside rim, leaving about 1 inch around the outside. Place the apple filling on the bottom crust. Roll out the other round of dough, place over the apples, and trim to the same size as the bottom crust. Use your fingers to crimp the two layers together.

Bake for 30 minutes. Brush with egg wash and sprinkle with sugar, and bake another 30 minutes, until the crust is golden brown. Serve warm, with ice cream.

# Buttermilk Ice Cream

MAKES ABOUT 1 QUART

The first time we made ice cream at Granny's house I couldn't believe how different it was from the cones at the burger shack. I remember my father filling the barrel with ice and rock salt. I was confused as to how that process was actually going to make ice cream. When he told me I had to turn the crank for 45 minutes, I thought he was joking. I had no idea that you could turn cream and produce a flavor and texture that was out of this world.

Kristyne Bouley, the pastry chef at Herbsaint, likes this eggless ice cream because it's easy and it really tastes of buttermilk and cream. The buttermilk provides the thickness that typically comes from egg yolks.

> 1 quart well-shaken buttermilk
> 1 pint heavy cream
> ½ cup sugar
> ½ teaspoon salt

Combine the ingredients in a large bowl or pitcher and chill for at least 30 minutes. Following the manufacturer's instructions, transfer the ingredients to an ice cream machine and process until the mixture begins to thicken and set up. Transfer the ice cream to a plastic container with a tight-fitting lid and freeze for a few more hours before serving.

# Lemon Meringue Pie

MAKES ONE 10-INCH PIE

Lemon Meringue Pie is the dessert my mother made most frequently, so it was a staple of my childhood. The peaks of the baked meringue make it look so dramatic. As a kid, this was pretty enchanting stuff, as in, *Wow, how did you do that?* For some reason I think of this pie as a summertime dessert, probably because the flavors are so light and refreshing. I've always associated lemons (and lemonade) with summer, even though they are really in season in the winter. Suffice it to say it's good year-round.

Lemon filling
½ cup granulated sugar
2 tablespoons all-purpose flour
2 tablespoons cornstarch
½ cup heavy cream
Zest from 4 lemons
Juice from 6 medium lemons (about 1 cup plus 2 tablespoons)
Zest from 2 satsuma oranges or tangerines

Juice from 2 satsuma oranges or tangerines (about ½ cup)
1 cup water
4 eggs, separated
½ teaspoon vanilla extract
1 9-inch Flaky Pie Crust (recipe follows), prebaked
1 tablespoon confectioners' sugar
1 tablespoon cornstarch (optional)

Preheat the oven to 350°F.

Heat the sugar, flour, cornstarch, cream, lemon and orange zest and juice, and water in a heavy-bottomed saucepan, stirring, until the mixture boils. Reduce the heat to low and cook, stirring, 7 to 10 minutes, until the mixture has thickened slightly. Remove from the heat and cool for 10 minutes.

Place the egg yolks in a small bowl with ¼ teaspoon vanilla and mix with a fork. Temper the egg yolks by slowly adding a few tablespoons of hot lemon filling to the bowl of egg yolks, and then working the yolks back into the mix. Pour the mixture into the prepared pie crust and bake for 20 to 30 minutes until filling is set. If you tap on the sides of the pie the filling should just slightly jiggle like gelatin. If it is undercooked you will know because when tapped the middle will look watery while the outside looks set; the whole filling should move as one unit. Cool on a wire rack.

Raise the oven temperature to 400°F.

Beat the egg whites on high speed until stiff peaks form, adding the confectioners' sugar and remaining ¼ teaspoon vanilla toward the end. (You can also add the cornstarch to help stabilize the meringue.)

Gently spread the egg whites evenly over the pie, touching the crust all around. Use the back of a spoon to make peaks, gently placing it against the meringue and pulling up quickly.

Bake the meringue for 5 to 10 minutes, or until the top starts to turn golden brown. Serve this pie warm or at room temperature.

# Flaky Pie Crust

MAKES 2 9-INCH PIE CRUSTS

12 tablespoons (1½ sticks) butter, cold
½ cup lard or vegetable shortening, cold
3 cups all-purpose flour
1 teaspoon salt
8 tablespoons very cold water

Using a pastry cutter or your hands, work the cold butter and lard into the flour and salt until you have a mealy, pebbly consistency. Add the water and work the dough into a small squarel. Cut the dough in half and wrap and freeze one half for another use (unless you're making apple or another two-crust pie). Roll half the dough out until ¼-inch thick and drape it into a buttered 9-inch pie pan. Use the tines of a fork to prick holes in the bottom of the crust, then place in the freezer for 10 to 15 minutes.

Preheat the oven to 350°F.

Bake the crust for about 25 minutes, until lightly golden.

The crust dough can be made up to one day in advance. Cool completely before filling.

# Blueberry Ice Cream

MAKES ABOUT 1½ QUARTS

Fresh summer blueberries transform ice cream from simple to amazing, with a stunning deep purple color. This ice cream flies off the menu at Cochon—it's a dazzling partner to apple pie or on its own. As a finish to a backyard cookout, consider using oatmeal cookies to make blueberry ice cream sandwiches.

| | |
|---|---|
| 3 pints fresh blueberries, rinsed and dried | 8 egg yolks |
| 2 tablespoons fresh lemon juice | 1 whole egg |
| 1 (14-ounce) can sweetened condensed milk | 1 cup whole milk |
| | 1 quart cream |

Puree two pints of the blueberries in a blender, then strain the juice into a bowl, discarding the skins. Stir in the lemon juice.

Slowly whisk together the condensed milk, yolks, and egg in a large mixing bowl, then *gently* whisk in the milk and cream. (For the densest, creamiest results, you want to avoid beating in too much air while combining the ingredients.)

Stir in the blueberry-lemon juice and the remaining pint of blueberries, then transfer the mixture to an ice cream maker. Following the manufacturer's directions, process the ice cream until the mixture starts to thicken. Transfer the ice cream to a plastic container with a tight-fitting lid and freeze for an additional 1 to 2 hours before serving.

# Resources

Duck (confit, duck fat, etc.):
Grimaud Farms
www.grimaud.com
800-466-9955

Heirloom pork (pork belly for
bacon, cracklins, etc.):
Preferred Meats
www.preferredmeats.com
800-397-6328

Sausage casings and supplies:
SausageMaker
www.sausagemaker.com
888-490-8525

Tasso, boudin, andouille, and
other Cajun meat products:
Poche's Market
www.pochesmarket.com
337-332-2108

Shrimp, crawfish, crabs,
oysters, and more. This site has
a listing of multiple suppliers to
order from:
Louisiana Seafood
www.louisianaseafood.com
504-283-9893

# Acknowledgments

A heartfelt thanks to the following:

My wife, Amanda, for supporting me in everything I have done since the beginning, and for all the other stuff that I can't even begin to write about.

My agent, Janis Donnaud, for seeking me out to write this book and showing me the way.

My editor, Pam Krauss, for getting behind this book and seeing its potential and for not pulling any punches when it came to feedback.

Paula Disbrowe, for helping me find the true soul of the book and keeping me on that path.

Chris Granger, for following me all around Louisiana to get the best shots. Sorry about the chiggers.

Special thanks to Patrick Dunn with Lucullus Antiques, for all the cool stuff for photo shoots.

Foster Creppel at Woodlands plantation, for a great location and some great meals.

Marysarah Quinn, for conveying my story so well on these pages.

Susan Spicer, for all she taught me.

Stephen Stryjewski, for partnering with me at Cochon and making it happen.

Kristyne Bouley and Brittany Casciatto, my pastry chefs.

Kyle Waters, Ryan Prewitt, and Warren Stephens for helping me test recipes and for running the kitchen while I worked on this book.

My staff at the restaurants for being the best at what they do.

Aunt Sally, for all the wonderful meals and stories.

My relatives in Cajun Country: JW Zaunbrecher, Loretta Kurta, Bubba Frey, Wild Bill, and Billy Link to name a few. They have been an inspiration for this book. Thanks for the crawfishing, frogging, rice tours, and Tuesday-night suppers.

Nancy Link, for being a wonderful person and reconnecting me to my family history.

My mother, for telling me my whole life to do what makes me happy.

My in-laws, Bill Hammack and Janice Parmalee, for helping me get the restaurants started and for endless good advice.

My dad, for all the good times at the camp.

And to my grandad, for being my true inspiration for cooking.

# INDEX